Learning to Love

OURSELVES

Book Two

P9-CEM-525

The Learning to Love Series

Small Group Bible Study on
Living the Christian Faith

by Richard Peace

NAVPRESS ◢
BRINGING TRUTH TO LIFE
NavPress Publishing Group
P.O. Box 35001, Colorado Springs, Colorado 80935

Pilgrimage Publishing, Hamilton, Massachusetts

This book is based on an earlier book by the author: *Learning to Love: Book Two. Learning to Love Ourselves,* ©1968 published by Zondervan Publishing House and InterVarsity Press. It has been substantially revised and expanded from the earlier edition and its format and focus have been altered.

ISBN 08910-98429

Cover illustration: Bob Fuller Creative

3 4 5 6 7 8 9 10 11 12 13 14 15 16 17/99 98 97 96 95

To Judith,
of course,
once again

Introduction

Chapters

Appendix

—————————

The LEARNING TO LOVE series:

Book One: Learning to Love God
Book Two: Learning to Love Ourselves
Book Three: Learning to Love Others

The aim of any Bible study ought to be to bring the reader into contact with Scripture in such a way that his or her life will be changed. This is my aim in *LEARNING TO LOVE*. The focus, therefore, is not on learning doctrine but on learning how to live like a Christian. Doctrine is present, of course, but always in relationship to life.

These studies were written originally in the 1960s to serve as follow-up literature in evangelistic missions conducted by African Enterprise, a group which I helped start while a student at Fuller Theological Seminary and with which I served for eight years in Africa. In their original form, they were published by two presses: Zondervan Publishing House and InterVarsity Press. They went through over twenty editions and were translated into Chinese, Spanish, Portuguese, and Korean. Certain parts of the series were translated into Zulu and Sotho.

But the original *LEARNING TO LOVE* has been out of print for many years. However, I kept getting requests for the books since it seems that nothing quite replaced them. The need remained to assist new Christians in beginning their lives as followers of Jesus. So it seemed appropriate to revise and update *LEARNING TO LOVE* as the inaugural volumes for our new publishing house: Pilgrimage Publishing.

When I first conceived of this project, what I had in mind was a modest updating of the original books coupled with translation from individual studies into a small group format. Of course, as I started working on the project it soon became evident that what was demanded was a thorough-going revision. The result is that only a small part of the original material remains. Most of the original topics are still addressed, generally using the same passages from the Bible, however in different ways. In addition, six new Bible studies have been written (expanding the series from fifteen to twenty-one studies). The result is, I hope, a highly usable series for a new generation of Christians.

The first set of *LEARNING TO LOVE* books was written in South Africa. It is appropriate that the new series was also written in South Africa during my sabbatical from Gordon-Conwell Theological Seminary. I am grateful to the many people who assisted me in completing this new series, both directly and indirectly, especially all the folk on Morningside Farm in Winterton, Natal, South Africa, where I lived while writing. Specifically, I want to thank:

- ♦ Joan Reeve, who opened her farm to my family, giving us a wonderful place to live, and her father Cyril Gemmel, who always had a ready story or comment;
- ♦ all the people who worked on the farm and helped us in one way or another: Musa, Gertrude, Rosie, Mavis, and the rest of the Zulu staff;
- ♦ the young people living and working there: David, Jolyn, and Katelyn Reeve; Bass; Rob Mark; Joel Howe; Jenny and Jonathan Peace; and
- ♦ the unforgettable kids: Daisy and the three musketeers—Sbusiso, Thabani, and Phumleni; as well as the other kids: Sindi, Thokozani, Zanele, and Freedom.

I appreciate the generosity of the Trustees of Gordon-Conwell in giving me the time to write through the sabbatical program. And, of course, my biggest thanks go to my wife Judy, who has supported me through yet another writing project. "Keep it simple. Keep it useful," she kept saying. I hope I did.

Grateful acknowledgment is made to the following publishers for permission to reprint copyright material:

◆ *Mere Christianity*, C. S. Lewis (New York: Macmillan/Collier Books Publishing Company, 1952).

◆ *The Minister's Prayer Book*, edited by John Doberstein (Philadelphia: Fortress Press, 1971).

◆ *The Fight*, by John White (Downers Grove: InterVarsity Press, 1985).

BIBLE VERSIONS

◆ *The New International Version:*
Scripture taken from the *HOLY BIBLE, NEW INTERNATIONAL VERSION*. Copyright ©1973, 1978, 1984 International Bible Society. Used by permission of Zondervan Bible Publishers.

◆ *The Message (The New Testament in Contemporary English)*, ©1993 by Eugene H. Peterson (Colorado Springs: NavPress).

◆ *The Revised Standard Version*, ©1946, 1952, 1971, 1973 by the National Council of Churches of Christ (New York).

◆ *The New Revised Standard Version*, ©1989 by the National Council of Churches of Christ (New York).

◆ *J.B. Phillips: The New Testament in Modern English*, ©1972 (London: Collins).

Richard V. Peace

An Introduction to the Series

Becoming a Christian is an awesome step to take. In deciding to follow Jesus we are turning our backs on many of the attitudes, actions, and ideas that once guided our lives. We are turning toward the way of life shown us by Jesus. We turn to Christ because we discover that the "old way" was the way of death; Jesus offers the way of life.

In coming to Christ, we are often thrown off balance. It is like living in a fog and having a new and powerful light burst through to show us a completely new path to follow. This can be a disconcerting experience. We no longer know what to make of our old lives; we only barely grasp what this new life holds.

This brings us to the point of this series: its aim is to illuminate the new way of Jesus while helping us to reflect on our old life.

We will examine the key ideas of Christ's way: he gives us a new way of viewing the world around us—a way filled with hope and purpose. We will reflect on the new attitudes that characterize the new way, since Christ helps us to form a new affection. This changes how we view others and what we give ourselves to. Finally, we will examine the kind of lifestyle Jesus wants us to have: what we do matters, and (at times) Christ calls us to stand against the stream of culture.

We will do all this together with others—with some people who have been "on the way" for a while, and others who are just starting on the way. The Christian way was never meant to be a solitary path. The church is intended to be the joyous community of pilgrims aiding and supporting one another "on the way."

A word about how this course has been organized. The three books of this series are structured around the Great Commandment given by Jesus: "Love the Lord your God with all your heart and with all your soul and with all your mind and with all your strength.... Love your neighbor as yourself. "

In Book One, we will look at what it means to learn to love God. God is alive and personal, as present as our next breath. Yet God is also Spirit. Therefore, having a relationship with God is different from having a relationship with another person. We need to consider how one grows and nurtures a relationship with the living God.

In Book Two, we shift the topic from God to ourselves. We ask the question: What does it mean to love ourselves? This is a concept fraught with difficulties. Improper self-love translates into a lifestyle that is hedonistic, selfish, and self-destructive. But we dare not avoid the subject, because failing to love ourselves properly is also self-destructive. With low (or no) self-esteem, people become doormats for others, fail to use their Christ-given gifts, and have difficulty loving others. Jesus calls us to walk the narrow road between selfishness and selflessness. This involves a proper self-understanding, a larger dose of humility, and a healthy sense of who we are.

In the final book, we look at our relationship with other people. Christ's call is, at its root, a call to love others. Yet this is so often difficult. For one thing, others are not always very lovable; for another, loving them sometimes gets in the way of our self-interest. But we cannot avoid the issue. To follow Christ is to live a certain way. Behavior counts; lifestyle matters. But it's not all sacrifice and pain. Our greatest joys come from others. To be in a loving relationship with other people is to be alive and joyful.

A word to those who are not beginners on the way of Jesus:

So far, it would appear that these studies were written solely for the benefit of those who are new in the faith. In fact, they were written primarily for that purpose. But it's also true that those who have been on the way for some time need to be reminded of the fundamentals of the faith. Martin Luther stressed this to the clergy. He warned them against thinking that once they mastered the catechism (the statement of the fundamentals of the faith), they could then move beyond it. Instead, he urged them to recite the catechism daily as a spiritual discipline. He wrote:

> "As for myself, let me say that I, too, am a doctor and a preacher—yes, and as learned and experienced as any of those who act so high and mighty. Yet I do as a child who is being taught the Catechism.... I must still read and study the Catechism daily, yet I cannot master it as I wish, but must remain a child and pupil of the Catechism, and I do it gladly."[1]

There is something very powerful about remembering what lies at the heart of the faith. As Luther indicates, we can never master even the most fundamental facts. We need to be brought back to them constantly. In a real sense, we never get beyond the ABC's of the faith—nor should we. Thus, this series will be of value to the experienced Christian.

It is useful to have a study group that consists of both new and experienced Christians. Both benefit from the presence of the other. Both need each other in considering what it means to "learn to love." The older Christian brings experience and knowledge—years of seeking to know and live the faith, and this enriches new Christians. On the other hand, the new Christian brings freshness and wonder to this task—new eyes to see old facts in fresh ways, and so those who are older in the faith are reminded why they started on this journey in the first place.

Blessings on you as you seek to walk faithfully on the path to new life in Christ.

---

[1] Theodore G. Tappert, ed. and trans., *The Book of Concord* (Philadelphia: Fortress Press, 1959), page 359, quoted in Robin Maas and Gabriel O'Donnell, *Spiritual Traditions for the Contemporary Church* (Nashville: Abingdon Press, 1990), pages 167–168.

A Three-Part Program

There are three main sections to each chapter. Each section has a special function in the process of learning how to follow Jesus. Knowing the intention of each section will help you use that section to its full advantage:

- *Group Study:* contains materials for a 60- to 90-minute small group Bible study.
- *Study Resources:* contains notes and comments used in both group and personal study.
- *Personal Study:* contains a series of reflection questions for use by group members on their own during the week.

In turn, each of these three sections has various parts, which are discussed below.

Group Study

Small group Bible study is at the heart of this material. This is where you will learn, share, pray, laugh, cry, reflect, and grow—together with a small group of friends and fellow pilgrims. The Christian way was never meant to be a solitary way. It has always been a matter of community. The early Christian groups were not much larger than your small group. They met in homes, studying and worshiping together. It was not until the third century that special buildings were used for the gathering of Christians. So, in forming this small group, you are returning to the original way in which men and women learned to be disciples of Jesus.

Your small group study has several components:

❏ *Overview:* The first page of each chapter has a brief description of the topic to be studied and the materials that are presented in each of the three sections. This will give you a clear idea of what to expect and how to proceed. You will also know what results to strive for as a small group and in your personal study.

❏ *Beginning:* Each small group study will begin with a sharing exercise that puts you in touch with the issue that will be studied. This is a good way to begin a small group because it gets everyone talking. It helps to move you from what you were thinking about (or worried about) when you arrived at the meeting to what the text deals with. It also puts you in touch with the topic in an experiential way, so that your discussion is not just sharing ideas, but sharing your life. Most importantly, it allows you to share your stories with one another. The questions in this section always focus on life experiences, and they are generally fun to answer.

❏ *The Text:* The aim of the entire small group experience is to understand and apply a passage from the Bible to your life. You will study material from various parts of the Bible. Different translations will be used, so that you will become acquainted with the excellent variety of English language Bibles available today. Since the New Testament was written to be read aloud, you will begin your study by reading the text aloud. Words in bold type are explained in the *Bible Study Notes* section.

❒ ***Understanding the Text:*** Unless you notice carefully what the text says, you will not be able to interpret it accurately. The questions in this section are designed to help you focus on the key issues and assertions in the passage. You will also begin to wrestle with the meaning of the text. In this section, you concentrate on the passage in its original first-century context (in the case of New Testament passages). After someone in the group has read the passage aloud, take five minutes for silent study (in which you think about the answer to each question). The rest of the time is used for small group discussion based on the questions. Optional questions are provided for you to discuss as a group (when time permits), or for you to do as homework.

❒ ***Applying the Text:*** It is not enough to simply understand the passage. You need to apply that understanding to your own situation. This is the aim of the final section of the small group study. The questions in this section connect what you have read to how you should live.

Study Resources

The *LEARNING TO LOVE* series is enriched by various study resources that extend and expand both the small group study and your own personal study. Some groups will assign certain sections as homework to be completed in preparation for next week's small group. Other groups will assign these as follow-up materials to deepen the small group discussion. In all cases, maximum learning will occur if you take time each week to work through this material.

❒ ***Bible Study Notes:*** Assisting you in the study of the Bible is a series of notes that will give you the kind of information you need to make sense of the text: definitions of words, comments about cultural practices, background information from other books in the Bible, etc. In addition, each set of notes begins with some comments on how the passage you are studying fits into the unfolding argument or story in the book of the Bible where it is found (Setting). You will find entries in this section for those words and phrases in the text that are printed in bold type. The hope is that these comments will help to bring the text alive.

❒ ***Comment:*** This is a reflection on the meaning of the text. A key idea in the text will be highlighted, or there will be additional information about some aspect of the text. Sometimes connections are made between the text and your personal circumstances. This section is usually written by the author of the small group study; it may also include selections from the writings of other Christian authors.

Personal Study

❒ ***The Art of Bible Study:*** In each chapter, one particular aspect of the process of Bible study will be highlighted. The hope is that over the course of the twenty-one studies, you will become a proficient Bible student, able to understand and apply the text on your own. In *Learning to Love God,* the process of observation will be discussed. In *Learning to Love Ourselves,* the process of interpretation will be the focus. And in *Learning to Love Others,* the process of application will be highlighted.

❐ *Extra Reading:* Exploring the world of faith is exciting. It will lead you in many directions. The hope is that these studies will pinpoint the key issues involved in learning to live a life of faith. However, the studies can only introduce various topics. You may find that certain issues interest you, and you will want to explore these in more depth. The books listed here will guide your further exploration. Of course, you will not be able to read all the books listed; however, you should try to read some of them.

❐ *Reflection Questions:* Based on the text you have studied, certain questions will be asked to guide your personal reflections in this section. It is best used as a way to respond on a personal level to the insights that emerged in the small group study. Generally, there is no "right answer" to these questions— only the answer that expresses your own thoughts, feelings, and experience. Sometimes your response will be brief; other times it will be extensive.

❐ *Journal:* The process of journaling is a helpful exercise that promotes spiritual growth. You may not have enough room on this page for all of your thoughts, so you will probably have to let your writing flow over into another journal. In fact, you may want to put all of your reflections in a private journal (so you can freely express what you are thinking and feeling), and use this section to jot down notes about things to share with the group next week.

The Appendix

❐ *The Art of Leadership: Brief Reflections on How to Lead a Small Group:* Almost anyone can lead this small group Bible study successfully—provided they have some sense of how small groups operate and what the function of the small group leader is. This is the aim of this section. It provides a brief overview of how to lead the *LEARNING TO LOVE* small group.

❐ *Small Group Leader's Guide: Notes on Each Session:* In this section, detailed information is given for each small group session. The small group leader should review this material in preparation for each session.

Questions About the Study Guide

Since this book is not designed to be read by an individual on his or her own, but as a guide for small group and personal study, it is important to explain how it is intended to be used. The following questions will give some idea about the various possibilities that exist for this material.

Who is this material designed for?

▶ New Christians who want to learn what it means to follow Jesus as his disciple

▶ All Christians who want to review the fundamentals of the faith

▶ Interested seekers who want to explore the Christian way

What is it about?

▶ What is involved in being a follower of Jesus:
  • How one meets and knows God
  • The spiritual disciplines of Bible study, prayer, and worship
  • What it means to be a spiritual pilgrim, walking in the way of God

▶ Growing and nurturing the Christian life

What are the distinctive features of this series?

▶ These are spelled out in *What It's All About: An Introduction to the Series* and in *How It Works: A Three-Part Program.*

How do I form a group?

▶ Invite a group of (up to) twelve people to your house.

▶ Start with a potluck supper.

▶ After supper, explain the nature of the course.

▶ Give a study guide to each person.

▶ Then do the first session together.

▶ Agree to meet together for six more sessions.

Why should I belong to a group?

▶ It will help you to mature in your Christian life.

▶ Everyone needs the support of others in growing spiritually.

▶ This is a great way to get to know others who are on your wavelength in taking the spiritual side of life seriously.

▶ It's fun!

What if I don't know much about the Bible?

▶ This is the purpose of the small group: to learn more about the Bible together.

▶ The *Bible Study Notes* will increase your understanding of the Bible.

▶ The *Art of Bible Study* will help you to learn how to study the Bible.

▶ In any case, this is a small group for learners (not experts).

Can a church run these sessions?

▶ Sure! This material can be used in many different ways:
  • with new Christians   • in a new members' class
  • in a Sunday school class   • at a weekend retreat
  • in one-on-one discipling

▶ Either the church staff or lay leadership can organize it.

How often should we meet?
▶ Once a week is best.
▶ Once every other week works well, too.
▶ Do all the sessions at two consecutive Saturday seminars (9:00 a.m – 1:00 p.m.).
▶ Or do all seven sessions at a weekend retreat.

How long should we meet?
▶ You need at least an hour per session.
▶ Ninety minutes is best—this gives time for more discussion.
▶ Some groups may want to meet for two hours:
  • This would allow more time for sharing.
  • Members could share from their *Journal* reflections.
  • You could also give time for personal study.
  • You could work through the *Study Resources.*

What if we only have 50 minutes?
▶ Take 15 minutes to do the *Beginning* section all together.
  • You may have time for only two of the three questions.
▶ Then split up into sub-groups of four each for the Bible study.
▶ Reserve the last five minutes for the sub-groups to come back together.
  • Then the leader can give a concluding summary.
  • Or the sub-groups can report on what they learned.

Where should we meet?
▶ In a home is best (since everybody is comfortable in a home).
▶ But anywhere will work as long as:
  • You can all sit around in a circle facing each other.

What do we do when we meet?
▶ Each small group session has three parts to it:
  • *Beginning:* in which you share personal stories
  • *Understanding the Text:* in which you dig into what the text means
  • *Applying the Text:* in which you let the text speak to you personally

What if we don't have enough time to cover all this?
▶ Don't try to discuss all the questions (the leader will select the key ones).
▶ Break up into sub-groups of four to allow more interaction time for each person.
▶ Best of all: expand the time of each session from 60 to 90 minutes.

Will we have enough questions for a 90-minute discussion?
▶ Generally you will, but if you don't, you can use the *Optional Questions* and *Exercises.*
▶ The *Optional Questions* can also be assigned for homework.
▶ The advantage of more time is that the open-ended questions can be discussed more thoroughly.

Is homework necessary?
▶ No, the group can meet together with no prior preparation.
▶ Homework does extend and expand the personal impact of the Bible study.

What is the purpose of the *Reflection Questions?*
▶ To assist individuals in applying the material in a personal way
▶ To facilitate recollection of the past and how it affects present spiritual growth

Can *Journal* entries be shared with the group?
▶ Yes, as long as everyone knows ahead of time that this will be done.
▶ In this way, not only will people work on their *Journal* reflections during the week, but they can select what to share.

What role can sharing *Journal* entries play in the small group process?
▶ This is a great way to tell your story to others.
▶ This deepens the impact of each lesson by following up the next week with practical applications of the ideas that come from group members.
▶ This brings the group into our decisions to change, and it makes us accountable to the group in a healthy way.

Who leads the group?
▶ Anyone can lead the group. Prior to the meeting, he or she must be willing to spend an hour or so to go over all the materials and to read the *Small Group Leader's Notes* for that session.
▶ The role of the leader is to facilitate conversation, not to teach or counsel.
▶ Shared leadership is often good. In this way, no individual can begin to dominate the group.
▶ However, certain people seem to be better at leading discussions than others, and they should probably be allowed to exercise this gift.
▶ Even in this case, it is a good idea to give new leaders experience in running the group so they can develop their skills.

GROUP COVENANT: every member should consider his or her responsibilities to the group and agree.

▶ **Attendance:** to be at the session each week, unless a genuine emergency arises
▶ **Participation:** to enter enthusiastically into the group discussion and sharing
▶ **Confidentiality:** not to share with anyone outside the group the stories of those in the group
▶ **Honesty:** to be forthright and truthful in what is said; if you do not feel you can share something, say "I pass" for that question
▶ **Openness:** to be candid with the others in appropriate ways
▶ **Respect:** not to judge others, give advice, or criticize
▶ **Care:** to be open to the needs of each other in appropriate ways

Chapter One
Loving Ourselves

At the heart of Jesus' teaching is the Great Commandment, in which we are told to love God and to love others. In the Great Commandment we are also told that the gauge by which we know whether we are loving others properly is self-love. "Love thy neighbor as thyself" is how the King James translation expresses this concept.

But herein lies the problem. Most of us are not very good at loving ourselves properly. We either undervalue or overvalue ourselves, and so lapse into self-loathing or self-inflation. Neither low self-esteem nor pride is proper self-love.

In this chapter we will seek to understand what it means to love ourselves properly. This is important. When we love ourselves properly—that is, when we have a healthy sense of who we are in Christ—we will not only do a better job at loving others, but we will also be freed up to use our gifts for God's kingdom. This theme of proper self-love will then be amplified in the remaining six chapters as we examine various aspects of who we are as individuals seeking to follow Jesus.

We will explore the question of loving ourselves through a Bible study in which we examine the Great Commandment, focusing on the nature of proper self-love (Mark 12:28–34); through an essay on the relationship between self-love and self-esteem; and by means of reflection on the connection between how we view ourselves and how we treat others.

The hope is that by the small group experience and through your own study, you will grow in your understanding of what it means to love yourself properly.

Beginning (20 minutes)

What a Cute Little Thing You Are!

How we view ourselves is connected to how others view us—especially how we were viewed when we were children.

1. What terms of affection did you hear when you were young?
   - ❏ Daddy's little helper
   - ❏ You're my love.
   - ❏ Good boy/good girl
   - ❏ Mommy's big boy/big girl
   - ❏ Way to go.
   - ❏ Well done
   - ❏ I couldn't have done it better myself.
   - ❏ Affectionate nickname: _____
   - ❏ Other: _____

2. When you were growing up, which person made you feel best about yourself? How?

3. As an adult, which aspects of your self-image can you trace to childhood affirmation?

The Text

One of the **teachers of the law** came and heard them debating. Noticing that Jesus had given them a good answer, he asked him, "Of all the commandments, which is the most important?"

"**The most important one**," answered Jesus, "is this: '**Hear, O Israel, the Lord our God, the Lord is one. Love** the Lord your God with all your **heart** and with all your **soul** and with all your **mind** and with all your **strength**.' The second is this: '**Love your neighbor as yourself**.' There is no commandment greater than these."

"Well said, teacher," the man replied. "You are right in saying that God is one and there is no other but him. To love him with all your heart, with all your understanding and with all your strength, and to love your neighbor as yourself is more important than all **burnt offerings and sacrifices**."

When Jesus saw that he had answered wisely, he said to him, "You are not far from the kingdom of God." And from then on no one dared ask him **any more questions**.

Mark 12:28–34
New International Version

Understanding the Text (20 minutes)

It is not easy to love ourselves properly. So much gets in the way: distorted perceptions, cultural norms that are destructive, bad childhood experiences, an inflated sense of who we are, a negative self-image, devaluation of our gifts— and the list could go on. And yet, as the text indicates, we are called to love not only God and others (which makes sense to us), but ourselves as well (which is hard to grasp). We will seek to understand this concept of proper self-love by considering what Jesus calls "the greatest commandment." As the text begins, Jesus is debating some Sadducees (members of a prominent and powerful Jewish party) on the matter of the resurrection.

1. Examine the text carefully by answering the following questions:
   ▶ Who approaches Jesus? Why?
   ▶ What is the most important commandment?
   ▶ What is the second commandment?

2. In what way does Jesus say we are to love God?

3. How are loving God and loving people connected?

4. What is the gauge by which we know we are loving others properly?

5. Why is the teacher of the law so pleased by Jesus' answer? Why is Jesus pleased by the teacher's response? Why were no further questions asked?

Optional Question

Jesus states that no other command is greater than the command to love in the threefold way he describes. But, in fact, other commands are more important in the lives of many people. What follows is a series of other "commandments" (guidelines around which lives are organized) that people make central in their lives. Discuss each of these and reflect on the moral, emotional, and spiritual impact these statements have on the people who believe them:

- ♦ "I'm number one and everybody better watch out."
- ♦ "In the end, the one with the most toys wins."
- ♦ "We are all dirt."
- ♦ "Might is right."
- ♦ "We are all gods."

In contrast, what kind of people will we be if we live by the Great Commandment?

Applying the Text (20 minutes)

1. Explore together the meaning of love:
   - ▶ What is the definition of the kind of love (*agape*) that Jesus is speaking of here? Contrast it with the way love is defined in our culture.
   - ▶ What are the rewards of *agape* love?
   - ▶ What is the price of *agape* love?

2. What does it mean for people to love God:
   - ▶ with their hearts?
   - ▶ with their souls?
   - ▶ with their minds?
   - ▶ with their strength?

3. How well do you do when it comes to loving God in this all-encompassing way?

4. In what ways does your commitment to God affect how you treat people?

5. Consider the concept of loving yourself properly:
   - ▶ What is the difference between proper self-love and inflated pride?
   - ▶ What is the difference between proper self-love and low self-esteem?
   - ▶ What are the dangers of overvaluing yourself?
   - ▶ What are the dangers of undervaluing yourself?
   - ▶ What is proper self-love?
   - ▶ How does proper self-love provide you with a gauge for evaluating your love of others?

6. Discuss the following assertion: Accurate self-awareness is key to proper self-love.

Optional Exercise

Divide into sub-groups of four. Give everyone 5 minutes to make a list containing five personal weaknesses and five personal strengths. Go around the sub-group and each share two of your weaknesses and two of your strengths. Then discuss:
- ▶ How easy is it for you to see clearly your strengths? your weaknesses? Why?
- ▶ What do you need to work on when it comes to proper self-love?

Bible Study Notes

Setting: This incident takes place during the last week of Jesus' life. It comes at the end of a series of fierce attacks on Jesus by the Sanhedrin (the ruling body of the Jews) in which they challenge Jesus' authority and seek to discredit him (Mark 11:27–12:27). It is striking that Jesus teaches about love in the context of such intense hostility. In this passage, Jesus reveals his greatness as a teacher. He combines two OT concepts in such a way as to offer the world a reformation in moral understanding. The love of God is connected to the love of others; and love is made active, not merely passive (i.e., reach out to your neighbor; don't simply avoid conflict with him).

teachers of the law: Jewish scholars who understood the meaning and application of Old Testament Law. In first-century Israel, they possessed great authority in religious matters.

The most important one: Literally, "Which is the chief (or first) commandment?" This question is typical of one of the two schools of Pharisees. We are most familiar with those Pharisees who sought to expand the law into thousands of commandments (in order to define how to act in every conceivable situation). The less familiar school (to which this teacher belongs) did the opposite: its members sought to reduce the law to its essence.

'Hear, O Israel, the Lord our God, the Lord is one': The *Shema,* a prayer from Deuteronomy 6:4, which pious Jews recited daily. In contrast to the innumerable gods worshiped by the Gentiles in the first century, this prayer states—unequivocally—that there is only one God.

Love: The love that Jesus urges here *(agape)* is an active, benevolent giving to others without expectation of reward. It is not based on emotion ("I do this because I like you"), on friendship ("I help you out because I know you"), nor on kinship ("I help you because I am related to you"). Such love is made possible by God's unconditional love for all humanity, which frees us to act in the same way toward others. Defining love in this way allows Jesus to teach that we are to love our enemies.

heart: A metaphor for the inner center of personality: the source of all thoughts, words, and deeds.

soul: The seat of the emotions.

mind: We are to have an intelligent love of God that engages our whole intellect, as well as our attitudes.

strength: The power of a person. The full effort of a person goes into loving God in this all-encompassing way.

'Love your neighbor as yourself': A quotation from Leviticus 19:18. In its original context it referred to loving other Jews. But in Luke 10:25–37, Jesus teaches that our neighbor is anyone in need—regardless of race, creed, or religion. Note that we are not *commanded* to love ourselves (as we are commanded to love God and love others). It is assumed that we will do so.

burnt offerings and sacrifices: These were at the heart of Jewish religion. In the Temple, where this conversation took place, countless offerings (of animals, birds, wine, grain) had been presented to God. The teacher of the law understood that God is most pleased by the offering of sacrificial love.

any more questions: The Jewish leaders had mounted a rigorous attack against Jesus following his cleansing of the Temple. They are furious that he, an unauthorized rabbi with a ragtag band of disciples, dares to challenge them right at the heart of their authority, there in the Temple compound. In confronting him, they first challenge him directly. They ask: "By whose authority has he done this?" (see Mark 11:27–33). Jesus gets the better of them in this frontal attack, so they regroup and ask him a trick question that will either land Jesus in jail or cause the people to disown him: Should taxes be paid to Caesar? (see Mark 12:13–17). This question fails as well, and so they turn to ridicule. This also fails to discredit Jesus (Mark 12:18–27). Then the question about the Greatest Commandment is asked, and Jesus reveals the biblical nature of his message and his unique power as a great moral teacher. This puts his enemies to flight.

Comment

Self-Esteem

Self-esteem has been a hot topic since the '70s, when the Encounter Group movement first emerged. We have been warned endlessly about the dangers of having too low an estimate of ourselves. Without strong self-esteem, we are told:

- we will never realize our full potential
- we will let others rule our lives
- we will not be happy
- we will never amount to anything

At first glance this advice seems to fit nicely with what we hear Jesus saying in the Great Commandment. In the Great Commandment, we are told that at the core of life there is meant to be love. This love is intended to be three-directional—extending to God, to others, and also to ourselves. The implication of this assertion is that if one element of love should malfunction, the other elements will be affected. So, the person who does not love God has difficulty loving others (because the experience of God's love frees us to love as we have been loved). And the person who does not love others is not loving God (because Jesus says that we show our love for him by keeping his commands, and the chief of these is the Great Commandment—see John 14:15). Finally, the person who cannot love himself has little ability to love others and, in fact, denies God's love (because he is hating one whom God loves).

But are proper self-love and self-esteem the same thing? Probably not. Certainly not in the way self-esteem has come to be understood in our culture. To be sure, self-esteem is legitimate and necessary, but self-esteem is often understood in a narcissistic way:

- which is self-indulgent,
- which is selfish and looks out only for that person at the expense of others,
- which is independent not interdependent, and
- which knows no legitimate boundaries or discipline.

What, then, is proper self-love? It is hard to define fully. But certainly, it involves:

- self-knowledge (seeing oneself clearly and accurately),
- self-acceptance (being who we are, not who others would make us),
- the ability to acknowledge the reality in our lives (as opposed to the way we would like things to be),
- the ability to face hard things about ourselves,
- the ability to accept success and failure in equal measure,
- the willingness to make the hard choice because it is the right choice, and
- the ability to get outside ourselves and see others as they really are (not simply as a projection of ourselves).

In the end, who we are must not be defined by a cultural concept of self-esteem. Rather, it must be measured against the biblical concept of who Jesus is and, therefore, who we strive to be.

The Art of Bible Study

The Process of Interpretation

It is important to notice what a text is saying. If one does not uncover what is being said, then all interpretation and application will be flawed. It will become more a matter of wishful thinking than biblical insight. However, it is not enough simply to observe what is in a text. You have to take the next step and wrestle with what the facts mean. What is the author seeking to communicate? What is his point? What do all the words add up to? We will be investigating the art of interpretation in the next seven chapters.[1]

First, some distinctions between the process of observation and the process of interpretation:

- The observation process is concerned with the *facts* of the passage; the interpretation process deals with the *meaning* of the passage.
- *Fact* questions can be answered directly from the passage; *meaning* questions require some reflection, and sometimes, research.
- The observation process looks at concrete data in the passage; the interpretation process involves connecting together various facts so their meaning emerges.

Second, the process of interpretation needs to be defined. Interpretation is working with a passage until we find its meaning. It is discovering what the author is trying to say to his readers. It is exclaiming: "Oh, so that's what he's getting at!" Interpretation is the process by which we penetrate to the significance of the passage.

Third, the process of interpretation involves looking for links between all the facts we have assembled in the observation process. For example, it is noticing that in 1 John, the author is identifying three false views of sin and contrasting these with a correct view of sin (1 John 1:6–10). Interpretation involves figuring out how a passage connects to what an author has already said up to that point in the text (so we see that John's understanding of sin is linked to his assertion in 1 John 1:5 that God is light and cannot, therefore, tolerate the darkness of sin). In other words, interpretation is putting the pieces of the passage together so we can say, "This is what the passage is all about."

For example, consult the note entitled "any more questions" in the *Bible Study Notes* section (page 18) to see how the passage you studied connects to what Mark had already written.

Extra Reading

The following books deal with the nature of love in general and with loving oneself in particular.

- *The Four Loves* by C.S. Lewis (Harcourt, Brace, Jovanovich). A penetrating and very readable analysis of the various sides of love.
- *Testaments of Love: A Study of Love in the Bible* by Leon Morris (Eerdmans). Another volume that helps us to understand the biblical view of love.
- *The Meaning of Persons* by Paul Tournier (Harper & Row). A Swiss psychiatrist with a deep Christian faith has written this exceptionally perceptive

book, which helps us to understand ourselves and our motives. This book can change you.

◆ *Escape From Loneliness* by Paul Tournier (Westminster). A companion volume that centers on the inner loneliness which the author says all people experience. Both books help us to know ourselves, which is the first step to loving ourselves.

◆ *Love Yourself: Self-Acceptance and Depression* by Walter Trobisch (InterVarsity Press). A warm, personal book in which the author shows the negative consequences of not loving oneself properly.

◆ *Our Many Selves: A Handbook for Self-Discovery* by Elizabeth O'Connor (Harper & Row). A series of exercises to help people understand themselves and then to grow.

◆ *Mirror Mirror on the Wall: The Art of Talking with Yourself* by John Powers (Twenty-Third Publications).

◆ *The Art of Learning to Love Yourself* by Cecil Osborne (Word).

◆ *The Art of Understanding Yourself* by Cecil Osborne (Zondervan).

◆ *Loving Yourself as Your Neighbor: A Recovery Guide for Christians Escaping Burnout & Codependency* by Mark Lloyd Taylor and Carmen Renee Berry (Harper & Row). Improper self-love can often be traced to dysfunctional family backgrounds. Berry and Taylor identify various faulty assumptions and unhealthy beliefs that foster self-hate and addictive behavior.

◆ *Learning to Love Yourself: Finding Your Self-Worth* by Sharon Wegscheider-Cruse (Health Communications). A number of books on this subject have been written from the vantage point of addiction recovery. They often have good insights, though they are not written from a Christian point of view and need to be assessed carefully.

◆ *Self-Renewal* by John W. Gardner (Harper & Row).

Reflection Questions

"Love your neighbor as yourself." This is very practical advice that is meant to change the way we relate to others. Reflect on how both proper self-love and improper self-love express themselves in the way you treat others.

Described below are four hypothetical situations. Imagine that each speaks about you. In each instance, two seemingly unconnected events are mentioned. How would you respond in each case? As you reflect on your response, look for the connections between the two events. The connection in each situation is between loving yourself and loving others.

▶ You just got your grade on an exam you took. You had studied hard and are pleased with the result. You meet your roommate who has received a letter from home telling him that no funds are available for next semester, so he will have to come up with tuition by himself. You say to him…

▶ You discover that once again you barely passed the exam and, as a result, your Dad reminds you how dumb you are. In the baseball game that afternoon, you are called out at the plate when you know you were safe. You say to the umpire…

▶ You have come to realize that the family you grew up in was less than per-fect. In fact, it was highly dysfunctional and you begin to see that the prob-lems you are having with your teenage daughter are connected with bad relational patterns you developed as a child. Over lunch, your best friend confesses to you that he has a drinking problem. You respond…

▶ You can't believe what nerds you have to work with. They are so dull. They never seem to do anything right. You are the only one who has any practical sense. At a party that night, you meet the sister of one of your coworkers. She is friendly enough and begins to strike up a conversation with you. You respond…

---

[1] A discussion of the art of observation is found in the first book in this series: *Learning to Love God.* The art of application is discussed in the final book in the series: *Learning to Love Others.*

Journal

_____

_____

_____

_____

_____

_____

_____

_____

_____

_____

_____

_____

_____

_____

_____

_____

_____

_____

Chapter Two
Valuing Ourselves

Overview

Human beings are quite amazing. We know this when we view the wonder and complexity of the human body, the astonishing capacity of the human mind, and the surprising breadth of the human spirit. But there is more than this to cause wonder. The really amazing thing about human beings is who we are in the order of God's creation. We are not always aware of the astounding value which God places on humanity. But if we can capture a sense of wonder as to who we are in the eyes of God, we can respond more effectively to the tough job of loving ourselves properly.

We will explore the question of how we are to value ourselves through a Bible study in which we catch a glimpse of where we, as people, fit into God's scheme of things (Hebrews 2:5–9,14–18); through an essay on what it means to live as people who are but "a little lower than the angels"; and by means of reflecting on what it means to live with a proper valuation of ourselves.

The hope is that through the small group experience and through your own study, you will grow in your understanding of what it means to value yourself properly as a person made in the image of God.

Beginning (20 minutes)

Angels

Except at Christmas (when they make a guest appearance), angels are little noticed these days. Still, everybody knows about angels, even if we pay little attention to them.

1. How do you picture angels?

   ❏ with wings ❏ as huge creatures
   ❏ as small beings ❏ as glimmering and shining
   ❏ as feminine ❏ with spears
   ❏ with thundering voices ❏ with soft voices
   ❏ as cute ❏ as awesome
   ❏ as protective ❏ as gentle
   ❏ in flowing robes ❏ other: _____

   Where did this picture come from?

2. If you met an angel, what would you do? Why?

   ❏ run ❏ ask questions
   ❏ hide ❏ take a picture
   ❏ worship ❏ try to wake up
   ❏ jump with joy ❏ other: _____

3. What do you know about angels? Where did this information come from?

The Text

It is not to **angels** that he has **subjected the world to come**, about which we are speaking. But **there is a place** where someone has testified:

"What is man that you are mindful of him,
   the son of man that you care for him?
You made him **a little lower than the angels**;
   you **crowned him** with glory and honor
   and **put everything under his feet**."

In putting everything under him, God left nothing that is not subject to him. Yet at present **we do not see everything subject to him**. **But we see Jesus**, who was made a little lower than the angels, now crowned with glory and honor because he suffered death, so that by the grace of God he might **taste death for everyone**....

Since the children have flesh and blood, **he too shared in their humanity** so that by his death he might destroy **him who holds the power of death**—that is, the devil—and free those who all their lives were held in slavery by **their fear of death**. For surely it is not angels he helps, but **Abraham's descendants**. For this reason he had to be made **like his brothers in every way**, in order that he might become **a merciful and faithful high priest** in service to God, and that he might make atonement for the sins of the people. Because he himself suffered when he was **tempted**, he is able to help those who are being tempted.

Hebrews 2:5–9,14–18
New International Version

Understanding the Text (20 minutes)

To love ourselves properly we need to understand our place in God's order of creation. This passage from Hebrews gives us a glimpse into who we are as human beings created in the image of God.

1. What does this passage say about:
   ▶ angels?
   ▶ human beings?
   ▶ Jesus?

2. In what ways does the quotation from Psalm 8 apply to Jesus as well as to the human race?

3. Explore what this text says about the role of humanity:
   ▶ In the first century, who did people think had been given the task of ruling the world?
   ▶ Who, in fact, has been entrusted with this role?
   ▶ Why do we not yet see humanity functioning fully in this way?
   ▶ What is the hope we have that our destiny will be realized?

4. How did Jesus rescue fallen humanity? Why is salvation needed for these wondrous creatures who were made a little lower than angels?

5. How can the kingdom of God be both present now and a future reality?

6. Why is it that Jesus helps "Abraham's descendants" and not angels? What does this demonstrate?

Optional Questions

Continue the discussion of angels which you began at the start of the small group session:

▶ What new insights about angels have you now developed?

▶ What new insights about human beings do you gather from realizing they are "a little lower than angels"?

▶ How would everyday life change if all people lived as beings made just a little lower than angels?

Applying the Text (20 minutes)

1. What does it mean to our self-image (and to the way we live) that human beings are:
   ▶ rulers of the world to come?
   ▶ "a little lower than angels"?
   ▶ "crowned [by God] with glory and honor"?
   ▶ members of the family of God and brothers and sisters of Jesus?

2. God has "put everything under [our] feet" and "left nothing that is not subject to [us]." This being the case, how should we relate to the earth and all that is in it?

3. Why was it necessary, do you suppose, for Jesus to have become a human being in order to bring us salvation?

4. What does it mean to be "a little lower than angels" yet in need of salvation:
   ▶ in how we view ourselves?
   ▶ in how we relate to others?
   ▶ in how we relate to God?

5. Jesus experienced temptation (yet without giving in to it). This being the case, in what ways can he help us when we face temptation?

Optional Exercise

Divide into sub-groups of four. Then take five minutes and begin writing an essay entitled: "A Day in the Life of Someone Just a Little Lower Than an Angel."

Read your stories to one another. Compare and contrast what each of you wrote. What are the implications of these insights for the way you will live tomorrow?

Bible Study Notes

Setting: The people who received this letter (Jewish converts to Christianity) were struggling with the temptation to turn back to Judaism or to reintroduce into Christianity elements of Judaism that had been superseded by Christ's coming. The writer demonstrates the absolute superiority of Jesus Christ to all that they once knew. First, he shows how Jesus is superior to angels (1:5–2:18); superior to Moses (3:1–4:13); and superior to the priests (4:14–7:28). In the section we are studying, he concludes his argument that Jesus is superior to the angels. In so doing he also shows where human beings fit into the divine scheme of things.

angels: Heavenly beings who serve (among other things) as messengers of God. They were considered to be superior to humans; some people believed they were superior to Jesus as well.

subjected the world to come: It is to humanity (through the person and work of Jesus) and not to angels that God has entrusted the administration of the coming kingdom. The Dead Sea Scrolls say, mistakenly, that the archangel Michael would be the supreme being in the Messiah's kingdom.

there is a place: The writer quotes a well-known passage, Psalm 8:4–6, and shows (Hebrews 2:5–18) how this OT passage asserts Christ's superiority to angels.

the son of man: In the psalm this phrase simply paralleled the word "man." In fact, this may well be used here in this quote as a reference to Jesus. "Son of Man" was his favorite title for himself, a title that emphasizes his role as redeemer of humankind (Mark 10:45). The original psalm described humanity and its role in God's scheme of things. But in its use here in Hebrews, the psalm also describes Jesus: his Incarnation (when he was made a little lower than angels), his exaltation, and his ultimate triumph.

a little lower than the angels: In the hierarchy of God, human beings are only a little lower than the mighty angels.

crowned him: Humanity has been given great honor and responsibility. It is, in fact, Jesus who fulfills the vision portrayed in this psalm.

put everything under his feet: The author points to the ultimate destiny for humanity: looking after the earth (see Genesis 1:26–28). Again, this will be realized through Jesus.

we do not see everything subject to him: Because of sin, humans did not fully realize their destiny as rulers of the earth.

But we see Jesus: Jesus has been raised to the place of highest glory. Regardless of the way things may seem, Jesus is the ultimate truth.

taste death for everyone: Jesus died for the sins of humanity.

he too shared in their humanity: It is thus not angels but human beings who share in the kingdom of God through the work of Jesus.

him who holds the power of death: Satan holds this power (in that he tempts us to sin, and sin ultimately results in death).

their fear of death: Death is one of the deepest human fears. However, Jesus overcame death and showed that death was not the final word for him (nor for his followers). He has freed us from this fear.

Abraham's descendants: Jesus came to help human beings. He is our champion who crushed the tyrant who possessed the power of death—the devil (Lane).

like his brothers in every way: He identified fully with human beings—even to the extent of dying—so that he could save us. Though he did not sin, he took on himself the sins of humanity in order to redeem us.

a merciful and faithful high priest: A priest is one who represents others before God. Jesus became the ultimate high priest by becoming a human being and then dying for the sins of humanity.

tempted: As a human, Jesus experienced every type of temptation we know, yet he did not sin (as the author tells us in Hebrews 4:15).

Comment

Rulers of Earth

To be human is to be caught in ambiguity. On the one hand, we were created to rule over the planet in benevolent stewardship. On the other hand, we forfeited that right when our forebears disobeyed God, and left us as a flawed, fallen race which sees its potential but never quite reaches it.

But Jesus restored our lost nature. He came down through time and space and took upon himself our ruined flesh. Yet when he wore it, it was perfect again. Though tempted in all ways as we are, he (unlike our forebears) did not give in to sin. Then, in a cruel reversal, he took upon his perfect self the imperfection of all of us. He bore our sins. He suffered the death (both physical and spiritual) that was meant for us. He who did not need to know death died in our place.

The result was restoration. Ruined humanity was reclaimed. But it was not quite back to square one for us. The earth still bore the scars of our disobedience. From typhoons to typhoid, the Fall made itself known. Nor were we ourselves free from the Fall. Fear, guilt, temptation, injustice, ignorance, anger—they all give testimony to our flaw. Not square one yet—but the hint is there that one day we will get back there. In the coming of Jesus, the promise of recovery began. In the Second Coming of Jesus, it will be completed.

In the meantime, we live in the ambiguity. We know salvation—even when we fail to live within its reality. The phrase "saved sinners" says it all. Both are true: we are saved but we are still sinners. Best of all, we know the author of our salvation. He has made us part of his family. And with the help of our brothers and sisters we keep remembering what is true. We are heirs of the promise—true rulers of the earth; who perform their duties imperfectly, but are on the road back to responsible stewardship.

The Art of Bible Study

Interpretative Observation

The art of interpretation is not very mysterious. You have already been engaged in interpretation even as you made your observations about a passage. The reason is simple: you keep noticing things about the passage that do not fit into the neat categories that guide your observation.

For example, in analyzing the Hebrews passage, you notice the central place of a passage from the Old Testament. In fact, the whole passage is based on OT ideas. The author is simply expounding what Psalm 8 means. Obviously the OT is important to his readers. In fact, they are very familiar with the OT, so much so that he does not even have to give references. They know what he is referring to.

These are interpretive observations. They help you make sense out of the passage. So, even before you start searching out other resources that will shed light on your passage, pay attention to what you notice on your own. An intelligent, careful reader can go a long way in grasping the essence of the passage without outside assistance. Do not short-circuit that process by turning too quickly to a commentary.

But you probably won't grasp all of the passage on your own. A second form of interpretive observation consists of thoughtful questions you have about the passage. Write these out. They will guide your study of the passage. A good question is a meaningful insight.

For example, having noticed the references to Psalm 8 you might ask: "What was the original meaning of Psalm 8? In what ways does the author stick with this original meaning? Go beyond it? How would his readers have interpreted the passages to which he refers?"

Once you have questions, then you know what to look for when you turn to outside references to help you understand the passage.

Extra Reading

These books deal with the question of what it means to be made in the image of God. The last three books discuss what it means to be good stewards of God's creation.

- *How Human Can You Get?* by Charles Martin (InterVarsity). The author seeks to untangle the various ways human beings are referred to by science, experience, and faith in order to show the uniqueness and value of human beings.
- *What Is Human?* by T.M. Kitwood (InterVarsity). A comparison of three views of humanity: humanist, existentialist, and Christian.
- *Your Better Self: Christian Psychology & Self-Esteem* by Craig W. Ellison, ed. (Harper & Row). An excellent series of essays on self-esteem written by Christian theologians and psychologists.
- *Counseling and Self-Esteem* by David Carlson (Word).
- *The Self-Image of a Christian: Humility and Self-Esteem* by Mark Kinzer (Servant), 1988.

- *The Image of God in Man* by David Cairns (Collins/Fontana Library). This book is fairly technical and theological but fascinating in its sweep. A professor sums up a variety of positions taken on the question of who human beings are and shows that we are, indeed, made in the image of God.
- *What Is Man?* by Stephen Neill (Lutterworth).
- *Issues Facing Christians Today* by John R. W. Stott (Revell). Stott challenges us to develop a Christian mind on a wide range of social issues as part of our responsibility as stewards of God's creation.
- *Rich Christians in an Age of Hunger: A Biblical Study* by Ronald J. Sider (InterVarsity). This book (and the ones that follow) explore what is involved in being good stewards of God's creation, which is our God-given mandate.
- *Tending the Garden: Essays on the Gospel and the Earth* (Eerdmans), and *A Worldly Spirituality: The Call to Redeem Life on Earth* (Harper & Row), both by Wesley Granberg-Michaelson.

Reflection Questions

1. To be counted "a little lower than the angels" is a high valuation. What would your life be like if you really believed this about yourself? How would this change how you:
    ▶ relate to yourself?
    ▶ relate to others?
    ▶ relate to God?
    ▶ relate to the earth?

2. "To be in need of salvation" expresses another truth about who we are. In what ways does your "need" express itself:
    ▶ in relationship to yourself?
    ▶ in relationship to others?
    ▶ in relationship to God?
    ▶ in relationship to the earth?

3. What are the struggles involved in maintaining a balanced view of yourself that neither undervalues or overvalues yourself? How can you live as a child of God and a steward of the earth without forgetting that you are subject to temptation and failure?

Journal

Chapter Three
Understanding Ourselves

We are "a little lower than the angels." To be sure, this is an awesome assessment if ever there was one, but this is not the whole story. In fact, there is another reality operating in our lives that works against the wonder of who God has made us. The Bible calls the evil infection that taints all people "sin." To love ourselves properly, we must understand what it means to be creatures made in the image of God but infected by a virus that defaces and corrupts that image. Only then can we understand fully the significance of Christ's death for us.

We will explore the question of understanding ourselves through a Bible study in which we find a compelling explanation for the troubling fact that we are drawn simultaneously toward goodness and evil (Romans 6:16–23); through an essay in which C. S. Lewis sheds light on our two natures; and by means of reflection on our dual natures.

The hope is that in the small group experience and through your own study, you will grow in your understanding of your dual nature as a human being.

Beginning (20 minutes)

The Devil Made Me Do It

Kids are wonderful. They are cute, funny, and loving. They are also—on occasion—little devils!

1. What kind of mischief did you get into as a child?
   - ❏ skipping chores
   - ❏ soaping windows
   - ❏ reading after lights out
   - ❏ watching forbidden TV shows with friends
   - ❏ breaking things
   - ❏ telling "un-truths"
   - ❏ going to forbidden places
   - ❏ smoking (drinking, etc.)
   - ❏ other: _____

2. What was your favorite excuse when you got caught? Did it work?
   - ❏ The Devil made me do it.
   - ❏ My brother (sister, dog, etc.) made me do it.
   - ❏ Who, me?
   - ❏ I won't do it again.
   - ❏ Did I do something wrong?
   - ❏ Mommy (Daddy), I love you so much.
   - ❏ It was fun.
   - ❏ Other: _____.

3. What tricks do your kids (nephews, friend's kids, etc.) play on you?

The Text

You **belong** to the power which you choose to **obey**. This is true whether you choose **sin**, whose reward is **death**, or God, who rewards obedience with righteousness. **Thank God**, that though you were at one time **servants of sin**, you were able to respond honestly to Christ's teaching when you came under its influence. Then, released from the service of sin, you entered the **service of righteousness**. (I use an **everyday illustration** because human nature grasps truth more readily that way.) In the past you voluntarily gave your bodies to the service of **vice and wickedness**—for the purpose of becoming wicked. So, now, give yourselves to the service of righteousness—**for the purpose of becoming really good**. For when you were employed by sin you owed no duty to righteousness. Yet what sort of harvest did you reap from those things that today you **blush to remember**? In the long run those things mean one thing only—death.

But now that you are employed by God, you owe no duty to sin, and you reap the fruit of being made righteous, while at the end of the road there is **life for evermore**.

Sin **pays** its servants; the wage is death. But God **gives** to those who serve Him; His free gift is eternal life through Jesus Christ our Lord.

Romans 6:16–23
J. B. Phillips: The New Testament in Modern English

Understanding the Text (20 minutes)

Why is it that when we know the right thing to do, we don't always do it? We know how to be good parents, but then we explode over some stupid little thing our child does. We know that dessert puts weight on us, but we eat it anyway. We know that honesty is the best policy, but we don't tell our client the whole truth. We know that we should spend time in prayer each day, but we just don't get around to it.

This is most curious behavior. It is almost as if an alien principle somehow lives in us—something that rears up between the knowing and the doing. We want to do right but we don't. We do the opposite or we don't do anything at all.

The Bible has some very penetrating insights into human nature that help us understand our baffling behavior. This passage in Romans gets at the problem.

1. To whom is this passage addressed? (Notice how many times "you" and "your" is used.)

2. What are the two contending powers vying for human allegiance?
   ▶ What is the "reward of righteousness"?
   ▶ What is the "harvest" of sin?

3. What is the "everyday illustration" that Paul uses to make his point?
   ▶ What words used in this passage are connected with the idea of service (or employment)?

4. According to this illustration, to which power do people initially belong?
   ▶ What does it mean to serve sin?
   ▶ How do they get free from the power of sin?
   ▶ What does it mean to serve righteousness?

5. What contrast is drawn in the final paragraph?

Optional Exercise

How might Paul have expressed this same truth about human nature had he used a different "everyday illustration" than that of employment? Pick one of the following illustrations and try your hand at writing a brief story to express what sin is, based on this image. Then share what you have written with each other.

◆ Sin is like being controlled by an alien force.
◆ Sin is like a disease, an ugly virus that kills us.
◆ Sin is like a spring twisted tighter and tighter.
◆ Sin is like chaos.
◆ Sin is like a rogue elephant.

Applying the Text (20 minutes)

1. What does it mean, in this day and age, to be a servant of sin?
   ▶ What do you recall of your old life before you left the service of sin and started following Jesus?
   ▶ Were there areas of your life over which you seemed to have little or no control? How did you understand this at the time?

2. What does it mean, in this day and age, to be a servant of righteousness?
   ▶ What differences have you noted in your life (when it comes to the struggle between good and evil) since you started following Jesus?
   ▶ How well do you do now with these same troubling areas?

3. Paul says that we begin to move from the service of sin to the service of righteousness when we respond to the "impact of Christ's teachings."
   ▶ How did you view Christ's teachings when you first heard them?
   ▶ What struck you as true? worthwhile? difficult?
   ▶ In what ways have you responded to the "impact of Christ's teachings"?

4. In what ways do you recognize the urgings of sin in yourself? The urgings of righteousness?

5. How does the promise of "life evermore" help us to resist the allure of sin?

Optional Exercise

Divide into sub-groups of four. Then take five minutes and recall some things about your old life that you "blush to remember." (This is an extension of the first question in this section.) Decide what you want to share with the others. It can be very freeing to acknowledge publicly what bound and possessed you. However, different levels of openness are possible in different groups. Share what you feel comfortable to share.

Bible Study Notes

Setting: Paul has just argued in the section preceding (Romans 6:1–14) that the Christian is called to a life of holiness. The reason for this, he says, is that Christians are in union with Christ. He concludes that section (in verses 12–13) with a call for a revolt against sin because we have been given new life in Christ. In this passage, Paul advances a similar argument about sin and holiness. He points out that while we once were servants of sin (literally, slaves to sin), we are now servants (slaves) of God. Since a servant/slave is committed to obeying his or her master, we now follow righteousness and not sin.

belong: A contrast is set up between sin and God. Like slaves, we are owned by the one power or the other.

obey: To be enslaved to sin is to follow the way of moral degradation. To be enslaved to God is to obey him in the way of goodness. If, in fact, we continue sinning, it is evidence that sin is our real master. Note that no third way is offered here.

sin: The Bible uses various words to express this concept. One set of words has to do with law-breaking: to sin is to do what is forbidden, illegal, wrong, or destructive. Another set of words portrays sin as failure: to sin is to fall short of what is best; it is to miss the mark, fail, or not to do what we ought to do. The first set of words portrays sin as active wrongdoing; the second set as inactive failure. Both describe the human condition: we are always unable to do what is right.

death: The end result of serving sin as our master is death—not just physical death, but spiritual death as well. Sin moves a person out of the orbit of God, both in this life and in the life to come.

Thank God: In a prayer-like statement, Paul thanks God that his readers have transferred their allegiance from sin to God. This is conversion.

servants of sin: A metaphor that expresses the fact that in the pre-Christian state, a person is dominated by sin as a slave is dominated by his master. This is not to say that one never chooses good, but rather to say that the overall direction of one's life is toward sin.

service of righteousness: In becoming a believer, you change masters. Whereas once you served sin, now you serve God and the cause of goodness.

everyday illustration: Paul apologizes for using an imperfect analogy, but he is struggling to make his point clear and understandable.

vice and wickedness: Paul began his letter to the Romans with a graphic and awful glimpse of the evil to which first-century pagans had given themselves over (see Romans 1:18–31).

for the purpose of becoming really good: In contrast, in giving themselves over to God, the believers' whole purpose changed. Instead of a downward spiral into evil, they experienced an upward spiral toward goodness. The word used here in Greek is "holiness" or "sanctification," and expresses the idea of becoming ever more closely conformed to God's way. The way of sanctification is the theme of Romans 5–8.

blush to remember: Some things people did before they followed Jesus are profoundly embarrassing.

life for evermore: Just as employees of sin receive death as their wages, those in God's service receive eternal life as the result of their commitment.

pays/gives: Sin pays out death as the well-earned wage of a life of wickedness, but God freely gives eternal life to his servants. One cannot earn eternal life; one can receive it only as a gift from God.

Comment

Two Kinds of Life   *by C. S. Lewis*

The Son of God became a man to enable men to become sons of God. We do not know—anyway, I do not know—how things would have worked if the human race had never rebelled against God and joined the enemy. Perhaps every man would have been "in Christ," would have shared the life of the Son of God, from the moment he was born. Perhaps the Bios or natural life would have been drawn up into the Zoe, the uncreated life, at once and as a matter of course. But that is guesswork. You and I are concerned with the way things work now.

And the present state of things is this. The two kinds of life are now not only different (they would always have been that) but actually opposed. The natural life in each of us is something self-centered, something that wants to be petted and admired, to take advantage of other lives, to exploit the whole universe. And especially it wants to be left to itself: to keep well away from anything better or stronger or higher than it, anything that might make it feel small. It is afraid of the light and air of the spiritual world, just as people who have been brought up to be dirty are afraid of a bath. And in a sense it is quite right. It knows that if the spiritual life gets hold of it, all its self-centeredness and self-will are going to be killed and it is ready to fight tooth and nail to avoid that.

Did you ever think, when you were a child, what fun it would be if your toys could come to life? Well suppose you could really have brought them to life. Imagine turning a tin soldier into a real little man. It would involve turning the tin into flesh. And suppose the tin soldier did not like it. He is not interested in flesh; all he sees is that the tin is being spoilt. He thinks you are killing him. He will do everything he can to prevent you. He will not be made into a man if he can help it....

The real Son of God is at your side. He is beginning to turn you into the same kind of thing as Himself. He is beginning, so to speak, to "inject" His kind of life and thought, His Zoe, into you; beginning to turn the tin soldier into a live man. The part of you that does not like it is the part that is still tin.[1]

The Art of Bible Study

Using Bible Study Notes

There comes a point in Bible study when you need outside help. You have worked with the text; you see what is there; you have tried to make sense out of the passage; and you have developed a list of questions about the text. Now you need answers to your questions. It is time to enlist outside aid.

In fact, you have already been using help. Following each Bible passage in this book, there is a section entitled *Bible Study Notes*. Have you noticed the characteristics of these notes?

- They always begin with the setting of the passage. These comments seek to put you in touch with what the author has already said in his letter, Gospel, etc. It is important to know this, since books of the Bible have a beginning, a middle, and an end. To attempt to analyze a passage in the middle of the book without knowing what the author has said up to that point is to invite misunderstanding.
- Then what follows are notes that give you information about the background of the passage. These notes include definitions of difficult words, descriptions of customs of that day, explanations of unusual or difficult concepts, parallels with other parts of the Bible, insights into the point the author is trying to make, and the historical context of the passage.

You will find other kinds of study aids in Bibles such as *The NIV Study Bible*. These include:

- Maps so that you can visualize a journey or see where a city is located.
- Charts that show such things as what the tabernacle in the wilderness looked like and how it was furnished; or the events that took place during Jesus' last week of life.
- Introductions to each book of the Bible, giving information about the author, the reason for writing, the main points which are made in the book, and the outline of the book.
- Cross-references to other passages so you can explore parallel concepts.
- Concordances that list key words and where else they are found in the Bible.
- Subject indexes that show where certain topics are covered in the Bible.
- Essays on important issues in the Bible.

All of these aids will help you to interpret the Bible accurately.

For example, see the comments on the word "sin" in the *Bible Study Notes*. The Greek and Hebrew words for sin are richer and more specific than the single English word. The explanation is intended to expand your understanding of what is meant when the word "sin" is used.

Extra Reading

These books wrestle with the nature and meaning of sin, and how we make choices as people who are made in the image of God but are distorted by a sinful nature.

- *Basic Christianity* by John Stott (Eerdmans). Part II consists of a clear, concise statement of sin and its consequences.
- *Whatever Became of Sin?* by Karl Menninger (Hawthorn). An eminent psychiatrist argues that the loss of the concept of sin has had a destructive effect on society.
- *Sin and Salvation* by Lesslie Newbigin (SCM Press). This was originally written for Tamil Christians living in India who struggled to understand the Christian concept of sin and salvation. As such, it is a clear, straightforward exposition of these important doctrines.
- *Mere Christianity* by C. S. Lewis (Macmillan). In this best-selling and very readable examination of what lies at the heart of the Christian faith, Lewis (who was a professor at Cambridge University) discusses Christian behavior in part III.
- *From Sin to Wholeness* by Brian Grant (Westminster).
- *Choices: Making the Right Decision in a Complex World* (Harper & Row), 1986; and *Mere Morality: What God Expects from Ordinary People* (Eerdmans), both by Lewis B. Smedes. Smedes has the knack of making morality readable, understandable, and personal. His books help us to seek to respond in a Christian way to the choices we face in daily living.

Reflection Questions

It really is like a kind of warfare—the tug between two opposing impulses. The one impulse pushes us in the right path, the other in the wrong path. And we don't always choose the right way. Coming to Christ makes a big difference, however. In shifting our allegiance, we find new power to resist the negative and do the positive. Explore this concept in your Journal:

▶ Reflect on the nature of the temptation you faced before you became a Christian. What was the appeal? What fruit did you reap when you gave in? Were there incidents in your life that moved you toward sin? Reflect on these.

▶ Reflect on the nature of the temptation you face now that you are a Christian. Where is the battle point for you? Where do you find strength to resist?

▶ Reflect on the tug of righteousness—both before and after becoming a Christian. Before you were a Christian, where did the impulses to the good originate? How do you nurture these impulses to the good now that you are a Christian?

---

[1]From *Mere Christianity* (New York: Macmillan) pages 154–155, 162. (Book IV, Chapters 5 and 7), 1943, 1945, 1952

Journal

Chapter Four
Behaving Ourselves

Overview

We are called to be "servants of righteousness." But what exactly does this mean? What is the pattern of righteousness we are to pursue? What is the lifestyle we are called upon to embrace? What behaviors must we avoid? What does it mean to be a "good" person? These questions form the focus of this session.

We will explore the nature of Christian behavior through a Bible study in which we find specific information about how Christians should and should not live (Colossians 3:1–17); through an "anonymous" letter from a "new Christian" that spells out the difficulties of living out a Christian lifestyle; and by means of reflection on our lifestyle, both past and present.

The hope is that in the small group experience and through your own study, you will grow in your understanding of the nature of Christian behavior.

Beginning (20 minutes)

What I'm Like

We all have our strengths; we all have our weaknesses. Knowing ourselves is the first step to growth. But sometimes our friends know us better than we know ourselves!

1. If a friend were to "evaluate" your behavior, what would he or she identify as your chief "virtue"?

   ❐ compassion   ❐ kindness
   ❐ humility   ❐ gentleness
   ❐ patience   ❐ bearing with others
   ❐ forgiving   ❐ a loving nature
   ❐ a peaceful heart   ❐ a thankful spirit

2. On the other hand, what might he or she identify as a "fault"?

3. What is one "virtue" you would like to develop to a fuller extent? Why? How?

The Text

Since, then, you have been **raised with Christ**, **set your hearts on things above**, where Christ is seated at the right hand of God. **Set your minds** on things above, not on earthly things. **For you died**, and your life is now hidden with Christ in God. **When Christ, who is your life, appears**, then you also will appear with him in glory.

Put to death, therefore, whatever belongs to your earthly nature: sexual immorality, impurity, lust, evil desires and greed, which is idolatry. Because of these, the wrath of God is coming. **You used to walk in these ways**, in the life you once lived. But now you must **rid yourselves** of all such things as these: anger, rage, malice, slander, and filthy language from your lips. Do not lie to each other, since you have **taken off** your old self with its practices and have **put on** the new self, which is being renewed in knowledge in the image of its Creator. Here **there is no** Greek or Jew, circumcised or uncircumcised, **barbarian**, **Scythian**, slave or free, but Christ is all, and is in all.

Therefore, as God's chosen people, holy and dearly loved, **clothe yourselves** with compassion, kindness, humility, gentleness and patience. Bear with each other and forgive whatever grievances you may have against one another. Forgive as the Lord forgave you. And over all these virtues put on **love**, which binds them all together in perfect unity.

Let the **peace of Christ** rule in your hearts, since as members of one body you were called to peace. And be thankful. Let the word of Christ dwell in you richly as you teach and admonish one another with all wisdom, and as you sing psalms, hymns and spiritual songs with gratitude in your hearts to God. And whatever you do, whether in word or deed, do it all in the name of the Lord Jesus, giving thanks to God the Father through him.

Colossians 3:1–17
New International Version

Understanding the Text (20 minutes)

In this passage, we find further clarification of what it means for us to have two natures as Paul describes the way of sin versus the way of righteousness. Paul is very specific. He strikingly illustrates the lifestyle that characterizes each orientation—urging us, of course, to shed the old way and to fully embrace the new.

1. In the first half of the passage (paragraphs one and two):
   ▶ What are the two opposing things to which we can give our hearts?
   ▶ What are believers alive to, and what are they dead to?
   ▶ What are the four commands Paul gives to believers that define the new way they are supposed to live?
   ▶ In what ways are the first two commands similar? In what ways are the second two commands similar? How are the two sets of commands related to each other?

2. In paragraph two:
   ▶ List the words or phrases that describe the attitudes and behaviors with which we are to have nothing to do.
   ▶ Define each word or phrase.
   ▶ What is God's attitude to these behaviors?

3. In paragraphs three and four:
  ▶ List the words or phrases that describe the attitudes and behaviors which ought to characterize our lifestyle.
  ▶ Define each word or phrase.
  ▶ What is God's attitude to these behaviors?

Optional Exercise

Try to construct a list of virtues and vices as defined by television. Think about how heroes and heroines are portrayed versus how losers and bad guys/gals are shown. Then contrast this list with Paul's list. What are the most notable differences in Paul's perspective versus Hollywood's perspective?

Applying the Text (20 minutes)

1. What does it mean, do you suppose, to be dead to sin and alive in Christ?
  ▶ How does this reality express itself in our daily lives?
  ▶ Why is there such a struggle to live out these realities?

2. Paul urges us to: (a) Set our hearts [and minds] on things above; (b) rid ourselves of those things which belong to our earthly nature; (c) clothe ourselves with the virtues of Christ; (d) let the peace of Christ rule in our hearts; and (e) let the word of Christ dwell in us.

   Which two of the following resources do you find help you most in your effort to put off your old nature and put on your new nature?
   ❏ Christian community   ❏ prayer
   ❏ small groups of like-minded people   ❏ Bible study
   ❏ worship   ❏ confession
   ❏ counseling   ❏ will power
   ❏ the Holy Spirit

3. Which is more difficult: purging ourselves of old ways of living or exhibiting new ways of living? Why?

4. Discuss the following assertion: Most of the behaviors that are listed (positive and negative) deal with how we live with other people. "There is no mention of virtues like efficiency, cleverness, even diligence and industry—not that these things are not important, but the great basic Christian virtues are the virtues which govern and set the tone of human relationships."[1]

How do these various behaviors affect (positively or negatively) our relationships with our:
  ▶ spouse? ▶ children? ▶ parents? ▶ friends? ▶ employer/employees?

Optional Questions

Paul describes here what the new Christian has "to learn about what he ought to be according to the plan of God" (J. B. Phillips). Becoming a Christian does not automatically make a person perfect.
  ▶ What insight does this give us into why an openly anti-religious person can be living a better life than a committed Christian?

  ▶ What challenge does this present to us as Christians?

Bible Study Notes

Setting: In this passage, Paul explains the secret that makes it possible for us to live in a new way. When we became Christians we died to sin and were raised with Christ to new life. When we grasp this fact we can then set our hearts and minds on heavenly things and (simultaneously) turn our backs on earthly patterns of living. In the first half of the passage (verses 1–11) he defines the old behaviors we are to flee; in the second half (verses 12–17) he defines the new behaviors we are to embrace.

raised with Christ: Paul begins by defining the new reality: believers are so closely identified with Jesus that they share in his resurrection life.

set your hearts. This is the first of four commands. When the New Testament writers speak of the "heart," they mean our inner attitude, motivation, and will. To "set" means to "seek" or "pursue."

on things above: The believer is directed heavenward, where Christ is seated.

Set your minds: This is the second command: believers are to use their minds to understand heavenly things.

For you died: In the same way that believers are alive in Christ, they are also dead to sin.

When Christ...appears: One day, when Jesus comes again to this planet, our true life with Christ will be fully realized in our lives.

Put to death: The third imperative calls believers to stop doing things which are contrary to the way of Christ. Paul goes on to name, quite explicitly, the kinds of anti-God behaviors he has in mind: sexual immorality, impurity (words that describe a variety of irregular sexual activities, from extramarital relationships to prostitution and fornication); lust (shameful passions that lead to wrong sexual behavior); evil desires (being driven by the desire for the wrong things); greed (lust for other people's goods); and idolatry (devotion to a false god).

You used to walk in these ways: With this phrase, Paul moves from describing worldly behavior to describing heaven-inspired behavior—even though he takes another paragraph to describe the old behavior!

rid yourselves: This is the fourth and final imperative. Believers are to strip off their "old repulsive habits" (O'Brien) like old clothes: anger, rage (anger is long-standing, smoldering wrath; rage is a quick burst of anger); malice (meanness; the deliberate intention to harm through slander or abusive language); slander (a verbal attack against someone, even God); filthy language (obscene language; filthy talk).

taken off...put on: The image here is of changing clothes.

there is no: Paul names some of the divisions that exist between people. These are all done away with by Christ.

barbarian: A general term for non-Greeks.

Scythian: This probably refers to the tribes around the Black Sea who lived at the low end of the social scale and from whom many slaves were drawn.

clothe yourselves: The believer must embrace a whole new set of values. Paul lists five moral qualities the Christian should possess: compassion (literally, "a heart of pity," the attitude of mercy Christians are to show those in need); kindness (to be warmly disposed toward others); humility (to be "lowly," not self-exalting or self-depreciating); gentleness (considerate of others and willing to waive your rights for their sake); patience (the endurance of wrong and exasperating conduct on the part of others).

love: It is *agape* love which best defines the kind of behavior to which Christians are called. It is love that binds people together.

peace of Christ: An attitude toward life that Jesus brings to the believer and which is to rule in all human relationships.

Comment

Confessions of a New Christian *Anonymous*

Okay, there are no more vague hints and subtle suggestions. We have gotten to the issue itself. This is how we are meant to live. We can't deny it. To be a Christian connotes a distinctive lifestyle and it is no good pretending that it does not. Paul is quite explicit. He lists the "sins" we are to avoid and he describes the "virtues" we are to embrace. Not that his lists are meant to be complete. They are illustrative—sample behaviors that give us a clear idea of what earthly things and heavenly things are.

Not that these lists come as any great surprise. We probably could have come up with a reasonable facsimile on our own. Christianity has been around for two thousand years and its moral code has worked its way into our culture. Not that we always follow it. We know it though.

And it's not that we have any dispute with these lists (though we might, wistfully, want to hang on to certain items on the "forbidden" list). We know that the good behaviors are good for us. They promote spiritual, psychological, and even physical well-being. A human being was designed by God to live this way. And the bad behaviors bring about disintegration, personally and community-wise. Paul is like a wise spiritual doctor writing out the perfect prescription for maximum health.

It's just that it's so hard. Take good, old-fashioned lust. It's an American thing. Look at our movies. Look at our magazines. Look at our lives. What are we going to do without lust? Temptations to impurity abound. And then there is the call to renounce anger and rage. What am I going to do without my temper? I'll never get the troops at work up and marching each day. And the ban on filthy language is going to make the locker room at the health club a quiet place.

Still, it is what I signed on for. My old life was a mess and all these new behaviors have raised eyebrows, I can tell you. I tried out "patience" on my secretary and she looked like she had died and gone to heaven. And trying to be truly loving has worked wonders at home. But it is going to take time till I get it right. Still, that is what I was promised—a pilgrimage, a journey. I guess I didn't realize it was going to take my whole life!

The Art of Bible Study

Using Study Resources

We need to examine with more care some of the resources available to us when it comes to interpreting the Bible. The more we know about such resources, the more skillfully we can use them. Study Bibles are good as far as they go, but if we are serious about our Bible study, we need more substantial resources such as:

◆ *Bible Dictionary:* Every student of the Bible needs a good Bible dictionary. This is often the first place we turn in the interpretation process. Having discovered the key words in a passage, the Bible dictionary then gives us their definitions. It also gives insight into customs, background into the ways a word was used, connections with other biblical concepts, etc.

◆ *Bible Atlas:* The Bible is a book of history. Hundreds of places are mentioned. It is important to develop a sense of where the major places are located in relationship to each other. This you get from an atlas. Also, the Bible spans thousands of years and maps change over time. A Bible atlas will show such things as Israel during the conquest, Israel in the days of Jesus, and modern-day Israel.

◆ *Concordance:* A concordance lists all the words in the Bible and where they are located by chapter and verse. So you can trace the use of a particular word (e.g., "heart") in the writing of Paul or all the references in Scripture to "angels." In this way, you can see how themes are dealt with throughout the Bible.

◆ *Greek and Hebrew Dictionary:* Most of the Bible is written in these two languages. Words do not always translate directly into another language (e.g., there are four different Greek words for the single English word "love"). So it is useful to be able to refer to the original words. There are certain dictionaries that are indexed to English but then deal with the Greek or Hebrew words. For example, Colin Brown, *The New International Dictionary of New Testament Theology,* 3 vol. (Zondervan, 1975–79).

◆ *Word Studies:* Some books trace the meaning of certain words or groups of words such as Ralph Winter's *The Word Study Concordance* and *The Word Study New Testament,* 2 vols. (Tyndale House, 1972, 1978).

Serious Bible students should have a good Bible dictionary, an atlas, and a concordance. A church library ought to have the other, more specialized resources. The important thing is not to have every possible study guide, but to have access to and know how to use a few basic tools.

Extra Reading

The books that follow deal with the related questions of Christian lifestyle, Christian behavior, and Christian virtues.

◆ *The Race: Discipleship for the Long Run* by John White (InterVarsity). As usual, John White writes with great clarity and insight as he discusses Christian beliefs, Christian witness, and Christian discipleship.

◆ *Christian Basics: A Primer for Pilgrims* by Dorothy and Gabriel Fackre (Eerdmans). This is an excellent introduction to the Christian faith. Chapter 6 deals with salvation and includes a discussion of the Christian lifestyle.

◆ *Christian Basics: A Handbook of Beginnings, Beliefs and Behavior* by John Stott (Baker). Part III focuses on Christian behavior.

◆ *Ordering Your Private World* by Gordon MacDonald (Thomas Nelson). When our inner lives are in disorder, we tend to be anxious and we have trouble growing as Christians. We need to learn how to put our inner world in order. This is the subject of this fine book: how Christians can organize their private lives.

◆ *New Life, New Lifestyle: A First Book for New Believers* by Michael Green (InterVarsity).

◆ *Consistent Christianity* by Michael Griffiths (InterVarsity).

◆ *A Long Obedience in the Same Direction: Discipleship in an Instant Society* by Eugene Peterson (InterVarsity). Using the Songs of Ascent (Psalms 120–134) as his basis, Peterson expounds on discipleship themes such as worship, service, joy, work, happiness, humility, community, and blessing.

◆ *Run with the Horses: The Quest for Life at Its Best* by Eugene Peterson (InterVarsity).

◆ *Called & Committed* by David Watson (Harold Shaw). Watson argues that Christians are called to be world-changing disciples of Jesus.

◆ *The New Pilgrims: Living as Christians in the Technological Society* by Ronald N. Hayes(Ronald N. Hayes, Publishers). A discussion by a New Zealand teacher of "how twentieth century Christians can maintain a simple, caring lifestyle in an increasingly impersonal technological society."

◆ *It's Your Life: Create a Christian Lifestyle* by Graham Tucker (Anglican Book Centre).

◆ *Called to Maturity: God's Provision for Spiritual Growth* (Herald Press), and Walking in the Resurrection (Herald Press), both by Myron Augsburger.

Reflection Questions

This passage is a challenge to reflect forthrightly and honestly on who we have been and who we are becoming. It is not always easy to face ourselves as we really are. But, before we can grow and change for the better we must first see what needs changing. Use your *Journal* to reflect deeply on who you are now, at this point in time, in terms of attitudes and behaviors.

▶ Go back over the list of behaviors and attitudes Paul says we are to avoid and reflect on each item. In what ways does it characterize you (if it does)? When have you done this or been this way? How do you struggle even now with this issue?

▶ Go back over the list of behaviors and attitudes Paul says we are to affirm and then reflect on each item. In what ways does it characterize you (if it does)? When have you done this or been this way? How do you struggle even now with this issue?

▶ In summary, what are the areas that you struggle with right now—both to avoid or to affirm in your life?

▶ Pray about these issues. Write out your prayers in your journal.

▶ Make a plan for dealing with certain issues. You may need to share your struggle with a friend. You may need to discuss the issue with your pastor or with a counselor. Reflect on how you can take advantage of the resources listed in *Question Two* in the *Applying the Text* section (page 41).

[1] *The Letters to the Philippians, Colossians, and Thessalonians* (The Daily Study Bible—Philadelphia: Westminster, 1959), page 188. See this section for a superb study of each word as to its meaning in the original Greek.

Journal

Chapter Five
Forgiveness for Ourselves

We don't always do what we know we should do. Our old nature wins out at times. What then? Does God get angry and reject us? Or does God demand that we undertake difficult penances in order to appease him? Or does God just close his eyes and pretend that nothing has happened?

In fact, God regards sin very seriously; so much so that he sent his Son Jesus to die for our sin. What God offers to us in the face of our sin is his forgiveness. We need to confront our sin and failure directly. In repentance and by faith, we need to reach out and accept the gift of forgiveness. Our Lord taught us to pray: "Forgive us our trespasses." We would not be urged to pray for forgiveness if forgiveness were not offered or needed.

We will explore the related questions of temptation and forgiveness through a Bible study in which we examine two short passages that offer valuable information about these two topics (1 John 1:5–9 and 1 Corinthians 10:12–13); through another letter from the "anonymous Christian" with more thoughts about trying to live the Christian life; and by means of reflection on forgiveness in the context of relationships and on the way you deal with temptation. The hope is that in the small group experience and through your own study, you will grow in your understanding of the dynamics of temptation and forgiveness.

Beginning (20 minutes)

Don't Tempt Me

"Everything I like is illegal, immoral, or fattening," so the saying goes.

1. Which of the following is the biggest temptation to you?
   - ❑ a double-thick chocolate milkshake with chocolate ice cream
   - ❑ an afternoon of golf (or _____) when you are supposed to be working
   - ❑ two weeks of solitude in the sun with people waiting on you
   - ❑ sleeping until noon
   - ❑ winning the lottery
   - ❑ denying you are ever tempted
   - ❑ other: _____

2. What is the best thing about temptations of this sort?
   - ❑ never giving in
   - ❑ giving in with good friends
   - ❑ learning to treat oneself when appropriate
   - ❑ giving in only occasionally
   - ❑ finding new temptations
   - ❑ other: _____

3. In our culture, what are the real temptations that give people the most trouble? Why?

The Text

This then is the message which we have heard of him, and declare unto you, that **God is light**, and in him is **no darkness at all**. **If we say** that we have fellowship with him, and **walk in darkness**, we lie, and do not tell the truth: But if we **walk in the light**, as he is in the light, we have fellowship one with another, and the **blood of Jesus** Christ his Son cleanseth us from all sin.

If we say that **we have no sin**, we **deceive ourselves**, and the truth is not in us. If we **confess our sins**, he is **faithful** and **just** to **forgive us our sins**, and to **cleanse us** from all unrighteousness.

1 John 1:5–9
Authorized (King James) Version[1]

Therefore let anyone who thinks that he stands **take heed** lest he fall. No **temptation** has overtaken you that is not common to man. God is faithful, and he will not let you be tempted beyond your strength, but with the temptation will also provide the **way of escape**, that you may be able to **endure** it.

1 Corinthians 10:12–13
Revised Standard Version

Understanding the Text (20 minutes)

Forgiveness is not some magic formula which, when invoked, wipes away the effects of sin and then allows us to go on doing whatever we please. Sin is serious business. We need to learn how to deal with it. This is why we need insight into both the dynamics of forgiveness and the dynamics of temptation. In 1 John, we find a clear statement about the nature and meaning of forgiveness. In 1 Corinthians, we get needed insight into coping with temptation.

1. Examine the structure of the 1 John passage:
    ▶ What is the central assertion on which the whole passage rests? What two images are contrasted?
    ▶ What are the four if/then (with the "then" implied) statements in the following verses?
    ▶ What is the contrast identified in the first paragraph?
    ▶ What is the contrast identified in the second paragraph?

2. In this contrast between darkness and light:
    ▶ What are the two false assertions about sin in the first paragraph? Put what is being said into your own words.
    ▶ What are the two true statements about sin in the second paragraph? Put what is being said into your own words.

3. Why is it impossible to have fellowship with God when we walk in darkness? With whom do we have fellowship when we walk in the light?

4. Explore how we receive forgiveness:
    ▶ What is it in God's nature that causes him to forgive us?
    ▶ What else does God do for us?
    ▶ On what basis are we assured of forgiveness?
    ▶ How, then, do we receive forgiveness?

5. Examine the nature of temptation as discussed in the 1 Corinthians passage:
▶ How widespread is temptation?
▶ How unique is the temptation we face?
▶ What restraints does God put on temptation?

Optional Question

A young unmarried woman was weeping in the office of her doctor, a woman, who had just told her that she was pregnant. "But I can't be," she cried, "I'm not that kind of woman." "Young lady," the doctor replied, "we are all that kind of woman." What was the doctor trying to say about sin and temptation?

Applying the Text (20 minutes)

1. What does John mean when he says that God is light? What are the characteristics of light? What are the characteristics of darkness?
▶ What does it mean to you to worship the God of light?

2. Discuss the dynamics of forgiveness (where sin has hurt another person):
▶ What is the role of the one who has done the harm?
▶ What is the role of the one who has been harmed?
▶ What is the role of God?
▶ How does the lack of forgiveness affect the one who has done harm? The one who has been harmed? Our relationship with God?

3. Give examples of the following:
▶ a temptation a person thought he or she would never face
▶ a person's strength to resist temptation
▶ an escape from temptation

4. What "way[s] of escape" from temptation do you find most powerful?
❏ being aware of tempting situations (forewarned is forearmed)
❏ Scripture (reciting Scripture drives out other thoughts)
❏ prayer (ask God for help)
❏ a friend (whom you can call)
❏ self-knowledge (of weakness)
❏ resistance (which gets easier over time)
❏ laughter (which puts things in perspective)
❏ commitments (which have no room for compromise)
❏ spiritual strength (nurtured over time)

Optional Questions

What role does forgiveness play in your life?
▶ How easy (or difficult) is it for you to ask for forgiveness? To forgive?
▶ Have you ever been hurt so deeply that you still found it difficult to forgive for several days? Explain.
▶ Is there someone with whom you still have unresolved business—where you need to forgive or ask for forgiveness? Explain.
▶ In what ways do you manage your life in order to "walk in the light" with God?

Bible Study Notes

1 John 1:5–9

Setting: This is a very tightly structured, symmetrical passage which begins with a central contrast (between light and darkness) and then spells out the implications of the assertion that God is light. It does this in four if/then statements (with the "then" implied). In addition, incorrect assertions about sin are contrasted with correct assertions about sin. Apparently, John is refuting the wrong assertions of certain false teachers. In John's prologue to his letter (1:1–4) he declares his hope that all may be in fellowship with God. Here he deals with the barrier to that fellowship (sin).

This then is the message: This letter, written by the aged Apostle John, sums up God's revelation of himself to the Jewish people. John makes three great assertions about God: God has come in the flesh (1:1–2); God is light (1:5); and God is love (4:8,16). These are amazing assertions and quite unexpected, given how the gods were viewed by first-century people.

God is light: To first-century Romans, the gods were capricious beings who cared little for people, and who lied and deceived. Yet the God of the Bible reveals that he is the God of truth and purity (which are aspects of light).

no darkness at all: The God of the Bible is not tainted in any way by evil.

If we say: John uses this phrase to introduce false statements.

walk in darkness: This error asserts that it is possible to be in union with God and yet habitually sin, that the way we live has nothing to do with our relationship to God.

walk in the light: To walk in the light is to be open and transparent, not hidden and dark. This is necessary for fellowship with one another.

blood of Jesus: It took Jesus' death to provide the way of forgiveness for our sin and the washing away of the blemish of sin (purification).

we have no sin: The second error is to assert that human beings do not have sinful natures.

deceive ourselves: This is more than a lie; it is self-deception (or wishful thinking).

confess our sins: John assumes that we will sin, but asserts that if we confess our sin we can (and will) be forgiven. To confess our sins means that we acknowledge our sin before God. Such confession is a sign of repentance (i.e., the decision to turn away from sin).

faithful: God will keep his promise to forgive us.

just: Forgiveness is more about justice than mercy. Jesus paid the price for our sin.

forgive us our sins: Our sin is dealt with—not by what we have done (which is to decide to turn away from sin, confess our sin, and ask for forgiveness)—but by the death of Jesus (verse 7).

cleanse us: Sin makes a person unclean; forgiveness washes away that sin.

1 Corinthians 10:12–13

Setting: In this chapter, Paul identifies various temptations the people of Israel faced: temptation to worship idols, to be sexually immoral, to test God, and to grumble against God (10:1–10). Then he discusses the dynamics of temptation. He reminds the Corinthians that they will be able to resist sin with God's help.

take heed: Israel felt secure in God's favor, yet its people lapsed into sin (as Paul has just pointed out). The Corinthians seemed to be headed in the same direction. Paul warns them that no one is immune from temptation.

temptation: To be tempted means to face a choice: the choice is to give in to what we know is wrong or to resist it. To give in to temptation is sin. Temptation itself is not sin. Jesus was tempted by Satan when he was in the wilderness (see Matthew 4:1–11). Hebrews 4:15 says he was "tempted in every way, just as we are—yet was without sin."

way of escape: There is always a way out for those who seek it. The Greek word used here describes a narrow mountain pass.

endure: God will enable us to stand up under the pressure of temptation.

Comment

More Confessions of a New Christian *Anonymous*

So what is going on? Do we need to be perfect to be in relationship with God? If so, I better pack it in right now. I mean, I don't even know all the sin in my life. I keep noticing new things that need correction. And even then I don't always get it right. If God wants saints he's got the wrong guy!

Still, I suppose that what he wants is for us to deal with known sin—stuff I see and know about (or my wife tells me about—she has radar for my imperfections). This is good, I guess. I need to deal with all that if I am to be the kind of person I long to be. Knowing that God forgives me is a powerful promise. This means that there is nothing I can't face in myself. God is big enough to deal with all my junk.

And this thing about not having fellowship with God when I'm walking in sin—that makes sense, too. There is nothing spooky about that. God is not withdrawing in an angry sulk from me. I am the problem. My mind and heart get clouded by sin. I don't think straight; I don't feel very pure (much less holy—but then I never feel very holy). So I don't get on with my relationship with God. I don't reach out to him.

But all I have to do is reach out. Confess. He does the forgiving. Amazing. And equally amazing: God is concerned about sin not because he is vindictive. He hates sin because of how it harms us. He really does love us. (And, of course, being pure light, it is literally impossible for God to tolerate darkness of any sort.)

No, it is temptation I have to master.

But what really gets me is not the obvious temptations. I have been fore-warned about things like lying, cheating, stealing, lusting, hating, and all that other stuff. I see it coming and I can generally deal with it. I turn to the Bible. This usually clears my mind and gets me thinking straight. If not, I call Harold. He sets me straight right away. No, what gets me these days is not so much my actions but my reactions. My boss hints at a new project and before I know it I have offered my Saturday even though I promised my daughter I would go to her Little League game. Or someone does something stupid and without even thinking about it, I lash out in anger. Or an off-handed comment is made about somebody and I join in with a bit of gossip. No premeditation. The old nature just flares up and flattens me. "Lord, help me bring my reactions into submission to you in the same way you are helping me bring my actions into line with your way."

Of course, I have to be careful with this way of thinking. "My old nature is the problem." That almost makes it sound like it's not my responsibility—the old "the-devil-made-me-do-it" line of defense. In fact, I did it. It is me—both actions and reactions. This is the stuff that is being redeemed, slowly, over time, by God. I guess we never lose the need for forgiveness.

The Art of Bible Study

Commentaries

Commentaries are wonderful and awful when it comes to Bible study.

Commentaries are wonderful because:
- ◆ They answer many of the questions we have about the text.
- ◆ In commentaries we find the fruit of research by gifted and committed scholars. These men and women track down data for us from a variety of sources and blend it all together for us in a useful format.
- ◆ They suggest interpretations we missed.
- ◆ They correct erroneous assumptions on our part about the text.
- ◆ They fill in the cultural background to the text.

Commentaries are awful because:
- ◆ They become a crutch for us. Rather than studying the text ourselves, we study the commentaries and rely on the opinions of others.
- ◆ They do not always answer the questions we have about the text derived from our own study of it. Instead, they often seem to deal with issues only of interest to other scholars.
- ◆ They make us feel as if we cannot study the Bible on our own.

A few more comments about commentaries:
- ◆ Not all commentaries are created equal. There are good commentaries and there are bad commentaries. Part of it depends on the view of Scripture espoused by the author. Some scholars have a very low view of Scripture. As a result, their commentaries debunk the Bible or deal with esoteric, academic issues that do not shed light on the text. There are plenty of reputable commentaries by able scholars with a high view of the Bible. Be selective in which commentaries you use.
- ◆ The Bible is the revealed Word of God, not the commentaries. Even the best commentaries contain, in addition to "assured fact," best-guesses, supposition, personal perspective, and inaccuracies. While no scholar tries to be wrong, it is just that he or she doesn't always get it right. Make the Bible primary, not commentaries.
- ◆ No series of commentaries is of equal quality. See *A Guide to Selecting and Using Bible Commentaries* by Douglas Stuart (Word, 1990) for a summary of what is available.
- ◆ Most importantly: only turn to commentaries after you have studied the text on your own and have questions which you need to be answered.

Extra Reading

Listed here are books about forgiveness and temptation.
- ◆ *The Christian Experience of Forgiveness* by H. R. MacKintosh (Fontana Books). A learned discussion of the process through which we know and experience the forgiveness of God.
- ◆ *The Cross of Christ* by John R. W. Stott (InterVarsity). A thoughtful, very readable discussion of the death of Christ and how this act makes forgiveness possible.

- *Forgive & Forget: Healing the Hurts We Don't Deserve* by Lewis Smedes (Harper & Row). Whereas MacKintosh and Stott discuss the doctrine of forgiveness and emphasize the forgiveness of God, Smedes looks at human forgiveness. In particular, his concern is with how we forgive those who have hurt us. Smedes discusses a four-stage process whereby a person can move from hurting and hating to healing and reconciliation.
- *The Fight* by John White (InterVarsity). This is an excellent book about living the Christian life. Chapter 5 discusses temptation. Chapter 9 deals with holiness. In it, White considers many of the issues found in the Colossians 3 passage. Chapter 11 ends with a discussion of the struggles of Christians to be all they are called to be.
- *Caring Enough to Forgive* by David Augsburger (Regal).
- *Forgive & Be Free: Healing the Wounds of Past and Present* by Richard P. Walters (Zondervan).
- *Lord, I Can Resist Anything but Temptation* by Harold Bussell (Zondervan).
- *Temptation: Help for Struggling Christians* by Charles Durham (InterVarsity). A most useful book.
- *I Hear Two Voices: Struggling with Temptation* by Donald Deffner (Concordia).

Reflection Questions

In the previous chapter, we reflected on our sin—past and present. In this chapter, we need to reflect on how our sin has hurt others.

▶ Go back over what you wrote in your Journal about your sin. This time, however, ask yourself: Who have I harmed by this lifestyle? Think about the important people in your life. What impact did your behavior have on them? What would you have changed in your behavior if you could? What do you need to say now to the people you hurt? Where are the trouble spots in your current relationships? With whom do you need to mend relationships? How can you do this?

▶ But you have not always been the one who brought harm. Who has harmed you? How? Why? With whom is there tension because of past wrongs committed against you? What, if anything, can you do to restore these relationships?

This chapter deals not only with forgiveness but with temptation as well. Reflect on your susceptibility to temptation.

▶ How well do you do when it comes to the common temptations: the temptation to power, to materialism, to lust, to control, to abuse, and to any of the other temptations you discussed in the Beginning section?

▶ Which "way of escape" works best for you when you face temptation? Think about your past experience. What lines of defense do you need to cultivate in your ongoing war against sin?

All of this is a challenge to us to keep close tabs on how we live. To do this we need to recall our activities each day. As we meditate, we begin to see what we have been like that day. We realize that sometimes we had wrong motives when we spoke. We may find we haven't been quite honest in some discussion. Or we may see that our behavior toward a particular person was less than loving. When we realize our sins, we can ask for forgiveness and receive it. Then when we have asked for forgiveness, we must accept it. Some people live with tremendous guilt feelings for years on end. Yet God has said he will forgive all of our sins. None are excluded. If you ask for forgiveness, trust that you have received it.

Here is a prayer that you might find helpful as you think over your day:

> Forgive my sins, O Lord—forgive me the sins of my present and the sins of my past, the sins of my soul and the sins of my body; the sins which I have done to please myself, and the sins which I have done to please others. Forgive me my wanton and idle sins, forgive me my serious and deliberate sins, forgive me those sins which I know and those sins which I know not, the sins which I have laboured so to hide from others that I have hid them from my own memory. Forgive them, O Lord, forgive them all. Of Thy great mercy let me be absolved, and of Thy bountiful goodness let me be delivered from the bonds of all that by my frailty I have committed. Grant this, O Heavenly Father, for the sake of Jesus Christ, our blessed Lord and Saviour. Amen.[2]

---

[1] The so-called *King James Version* of the Bible is one of the great English translations. It is not used as much as it once was, since its language is seventeenth-century English and the Greek and Hebrew text on which it is based is not as accurate as it could be. However, the poetry of the King James Version has never been surpassed.

[2] *The Minister's Prayer Book:* John Doberstein, ed., page 33 (Philadelphia: Fortress, 1971).

Journal

_____

_____

_____

_____

_____

_____

_____

_____

_____

_____

_____

Chapter Six
Growing Ourselves

Overview

Once we have understood who we are in Christ—flawed, fallen human beings made in the image of God and saved by grace—we can get on with the business of becoming all we are meant to be in Christ. In fact, this is our task for the rest of our lives: to grow in grace. That is the subject of this chapter. The Apostle Paul spells out the dynamics of Christian growth in a powerful passage found in his letter to the Philippians.

We will explore the question of growth through a Bible study in which we examine Paul's explanation of how change takes place in our lives (Philippians 3:4–14); through an essay on the awesome power of repentance and faith; and by means of reflection on forgiveness in the context of relationships, and reflection on the process of growth in our lives.

The hope is that through the small group experience and your own study, you will grow in your understanding of the dynamics of Christian growth.

Beginning (20 minutes)

The Power of the Future

When we are excited about the future, we have great energy to make the future happen.

1. When you were a child, which event could you hardly wait for? Why?
   - ❏ Christmas (or another holiday)
   - ❏ getting your first pet
   - ❏ your birthday
   - ❏ first Communion
   - ❏ school vacation
   - ❏ taking a special trip
   - ❏ going (back) to school
   - ❏ growing up

2. When you were a teenager, what did you especially look forward to? Explain.
   - ❏ college
   - ❏ a career
   - ❏ your own apartment
   - ❏ freedom
   - ❏ marriage
   - ❏ travel
   - ❏ a car

3. As an adult, what excites you about the future?
   - ❏ learning new things
   - ❏ getting better at my job
   - ❏ developing new skills
   - ❏ becoming a spiritual leader
   - ❏ going to new places
   - ❏ tackling a new challenge
   - ❏ realizing my creativity
   - ❏ using my skills for others

The Text

If anyone else thinks he has reasons to put **confidence in the flesh**, I have more: **circumcised** on the eighth day, of the **people of Israel**, of the **tribe of Benjamin**, a **Hebrew of Hebrews**; in regard to the law, a **Pharisee**; as for **zeal**, persecuting the church; as for **legalistic righteousness**, faultless.

But whatever was to my **profit** I now consider **loss** for the sake of Christ. What is more, I consider everything a loss compared to the surpassing greatness of knowing Christ Jesus my Lord, for whose sake I have lost all things. I consider them rubbish, that I may **gain Christ** and be **found in him**, not having a righteousness of my own that comes from the law, but that which is through faith in Christ—**the righteousness that comes from God** and is by faith. I want to know Christ and the power of his resurrection and the fellowship of sharing in his sufferings, becoming like him in his death, and so, **somehow, to attain** to the resurrection from the dead.

Not that I have already obtained all this, or have already been made **perfect**, but I **press on** to take hold of that for which Christ Jesus took hold of me. Brothers, I do not consider myself yet to have taken hold of it. But one thing I do: **Forgetting what is behind** and **straining toward what is ahead**, I press on toward the goal to win the **prize** for which God has called me heavenward in Christ Jesus.

Philippians 3:4–14
New International Version

Understanding the Text (20 minutes)

Paul describes what energized him in his pre-Christian days and compares it with what energized him after he met Christ. In so doing, he reveals to us the dynamics of Christian growth.

1. Examine Paul's pre-Christian religious accomplishments (first paragraph) by answering the following questions:
   ▶ What are the seven parts of his religious background and accomplishments?
   ▶ What does each phrase tell us about the kind of person he was?
   ▶ What conclusion would a first-century Jew have reached about the religious character of Paul?

2. Examine Paul's Christian experience (second paragraph) by answering the following questions. Notice that Paul states each of these ideas in more than one way.
   ▶ What is Paul's assessment of his pre-Christian religious accomplishments?
   ▶ Where does Paul now find personal righteousness?
   ▶ What is Paul's goal?

3. Examine Paul's view of the dynamics of the Christian life (third paragraph):
   ▶ What image does Paul use to describe the Christian life?
   ▶ What is his attitude to the past? the present? the future?
   ▶ What is his mid-race posture?
   ▶ What words does Paul use to express the dynamic nature of the Christian life? The goal of the Christian life?

Optional Exercise

Testimonies have long been a part of Christian witness. You have read Paul's testimony. Now begin to write down your testimony based on the following guidelines. After five minutes of work, share what you have written with the group.

♦ Describe what life was like for you before you met Christ.

♦ Describe what has changed since you met Christ.

♦ Be specific. Share incidents, not generalities.

♦ Be honest. To paint your past as all bad and your present as all good is suspect!

♦ Be brief. There is no need to share your whole theology!

Applying the Text (20 minutes)

1. Paul's testimony has two parts to it: where he found meaning and purpose before meeting Christ ("confidence in the flesh") and what it was like afterwards ("found in him").

   ▶ Before you became a Christian, what gave you a sense of meaning and purpose? What was genuine and what was wishful thinking about that?

   ▶ In what ways did your sense of meaning and purpose change after you met Christ?

2. Consider your attitudes about growth:

   ▶ How do you deal with your past?
   - ❒ I don't think about it.
   - ❒ I am exploring it.
   - ❒ I am weighed down by it.
   - ❒ I have no regrets.
   - ❒ I have some regrets.
   - ❒ I know on a deep level that I am forgiven.
   - ❒ I am confronting past issues.
   - ❒ Other: _____.

   ▶ What is your attitude to the present?
   - ❒ I do what needs to be done.
   - ❒ I am actively seeking to grow.
   - ❒ I need to start growing.
   - ❒ I try, but growth is hard for me.
   - ❒ I do not have many issues I need to deal with.
   - ❒ Other: _____.

   ▶ How does the future affect you?
   - ❒ Not at all.
   - ❒ I am motivated by what God has promised.
   - ❒ The promise of heaven is a great comfort.
   - ❒ I worry about the future.
   - ❒ I am excited about the future.
   - ❒ Other: _____.

3. Explore the process of growth. In what ways are you "pressing on" in your spiritual life?

   ▶ How does focusing on your past trip you up as you seek to grow?

   ▶ How does focusing on the future urge you forward?

4. Explore the goal of growth:

   ▶ In what ways do the various promises motivate you:
   - the promise of new growth (becoming what Christ wants you to be)?
   - the promise of the resurrection (heaven)?

Optional Exercise

Paul uses the metaphor of a runner to describe the nature of the Christian life. In what ways would the following metaphors be apt descriptions of the Christian life?

▶a pilgrim   ▶a soldier   ▶an explorer   ▶an ambassador

Bible Study Notes

Setting: This section contains Paul's personal testimony of why he lost confidence in his Jewish pedigree and accomplishments, and placed his confidence instead in the saving work of Christ. Paul begins by outlining his impeccable credentials as one who had attained the pinnacle of first-century Jewish spirituality. He discovered, however, that all of his accomplishments were utterly meaningless because only one thing counted: knowing Christ Jesus. He ends by describing his efforts to live the Christian life. In so doing, he provides us with a valuable insight into what is involved in nurturing our lives in Christ.

If anyone else thinks he has reasons: Paul's opponents dispute his teaching (that law and ritual are of little value) and claim he is not an authentic Jew. In response, Paul lays out his substantial credentials as a Jew.

confidence in the flesh: First-century Jewish spirituality focused on a righteousness that was the product of heritage and hard work. If you were born into the right community (and were one of the chosen race) and if you kept the law in its entirety, then you could be confident that God would pronounce you righteous on Judgment Day, and would welcome you into his kingdom. It is this view Paul disputes.

circumcised: Circumcision (removal of the male foreskin) was a sign of commitment to the covenant God made with Abraham.

people of Israel: Paul was born a Jew. He had not converted to Judaism.

tribe of Benjamin: An elite tribe within Israel.

Hebrew of Hebrews: In all ways—language, commitments, and lifestyle—Paul was deeply and unambiguously Jewish.

Pharisee: A small, deeply committed band of men who devoted themselves to keeping the Jewish law.

zeal: The most highly prized attribute among the Jews. Paul had demonstrated his zeal to uphold the law by persecuting Christians, even to death (Acts 22:4).

legalistic righteousness: The aim of first-century religion was to keep the law in all its detail and so earn God's approval.

profit/loss: Paul's life has shifted from being self-centered to being Christ-centered. Using the metaphor of a balance sheet, what was once on the profit side of the ledger has now been moved to the loss side.

gain Christ...found in him: Paul's goal is to have an ongoing relationship with Jesus, the only thing worth having.

the righteousness that comes from God: It is not earned. It comes by grace, having been purchased by the death of Christ for the sins of humanity.

somehow, to attain: Paul has no doubt that he will be among those who are raised to new life in Christ. His wording here is a humble recognition that such attainment is a gift of God.

Not that I have already obtained all this: Paul does not claim he has reached spiritual perfection. That would mean fully comprehending the magnificence of Jesus on all levels, and Paul knows this is an impossible goal.

perfect: Certain mystery religions in the first century offered their followers "perfection." Paul makes no such promise.

press on: The Christian life is the ongoing process of striving to know Christ in his fullness. This is the key to its dynamic.

Forgetting what is behind: We cannot run the Christian race if we are looking over our shoulder at past sins. Paul knew he had to leave behind both past failure (persecuting the church) and past success (attaining the pinnacle of Jewish spirituality).

straining toward what is ahead: Paul uses the image of a runner in mid-stride, straining for the finish line ahead with a single-minded energy.

prize: In Greek athletic competition, the winner received a prize of a garland of leaves, or sometimes, cash. For the Christian, the prize is heaven.

Comment

The Secret of the Successful Christian Life

Down through the ages, certain Christians have sought "the secret" that would enable them to live successful, fruitful Christian lives. In many cases, this has been wishful thinking, a desire for some magic formula that would produce instant holiness or perfection. But the desire is understandable because, in fact, there is such a thing as a "core pattern" for spiritual growth. It is not magic, though it does involve a mysterious conjunction of human and divine effort. Nor is it unfamiliar. You see, when it gets right down to it, Christian growth involves nothing more and nothing less than repentance and faith.

It works like this. We grow when we acknowledge areas in our lives that need to change (confession), decide to go a different way (repentance), and reach out to Jesus to make it possible to do so (faith). In other words, we grow in Christ in the same way that we became a Christian in the first place—by repentance and faith in Jesus.

Let's consider these two key issues in more detail.

The root meaning of repentance is "to change one's mind." But before we can "change our minds" about the way we are living or thinking, we must first be aware that a change is in order. Insight is like a spotlight. It shines into various corners of our lives and reveals what is really there. It does not matter whether the insight is negative ("something is wrong") or positive ("there is a better way"). The important thing is that we have come to realize that the status quo is wrong or, at the very least, not the best. Insight opens up the option of change.

There are two basic responses to insight. We can say "yes" or we can say "no." If we say "yes," and thus acknowledge that the insight is true, we have opened ourselves to the possibility of change. If we say "no," we choose instead to remain where we are and risk the deadliness of sin and stagnation. If repentance opens the possibility of change, then faith actually brings about new growth. Faith relates to growth in at least three ways:

First, faith enables us to face ourselves as we really are. Assured that God loves us and will in fact forgive our sins, we have the courage to face what is ugly in ourselves. We can look, without hesitation, at those thoughts, words, and deeds that need to be forgiven and changed. Without this assurance, our natural tendency is to shy away from the light that points out our weaknesses, or to deny that we have any problems.

Second, our faith defines for us the direction in which we ought to change. We accept by faith that the pattern for living set out in Scripture is indeed God's pattern.

Third, by faith we open ourselves to gifts from God that bring about change: the gift of fellowship and the gift of the Holy Spirit. Fellowship is powerful. On our own, we are so powerless. But in the company of a supportive group we gain the courage and accountability to change. In the end, of course, it is the Holy Spirit who gives the power that enables us to change. Countless people throughout the ages have testified to transformations in their lives that were brought about by a power they knew was not their own.

The Art of Bible Study

Tracking Down a Word

Having Bible study resources is one thing; using them properly is another. How does one track down the kind of insight that sheds light on a passage? For example, in the text this session, Paul says: "as for zeal, persecuting the church" (verse 6). At first glance, it is hard to see what he means. What is the connection between zeal and persecution? Why would he include this phrase as one of his old qualifications?

The process of interpretation begins by examining the word "zeal." According to the *New Bible Dictionary*, zeal is "fervor in advancing a cause or in rendering service." The entry goes on to describe the Greek and Hebrew words translated "zeal" and then it discusses certain references. None of this helps much. It does little to explain what Paul is saying. (Remember, not all your research will yield positive results. You have to keep looking.)

However, when you look up this passage in Barclay's commentary on Philippians, he makes the comment: "To a Jew zeal was the greatest quality in the religious life. Phinehas had saved the people from the wrath of God, and had been given an everlasting priesthood, because he was zealous for his God (Numbers 25:11–13). A burning zeal for God was the badge of honour and the hallmark of Jewish religion. Paul had been so zealous a Jew that he had tried to wipe out the opponents of Judaism." Now we know how "persecuting the church" would be an example of zeal.

In this light, then, we understand what Paul is doing. He is listing his qualifications from the point of view of the Jewish religious leaders of that day. From their point of view, it was a very good thing to try to get rid of the church. The church was leading people away from the truth of the law (in their view). So, a zealous young Pharisee like Paul might well prove his devotion by undertaking the somewhat daunting and unpopular task of seeking out and convicting Christians. Using references properly is an important part of the art of interpretation.

Extra Reading

These books deal with the theme of discipleship:

- *Finding Spiritual Direction: The Challenge & Joys of Christian Growth* by Douglas Webster (InterVarsity). Using the letter of James, Webster challenges us to live a Spirit-filled life in the midst of the complexity and hectic nature of ordinary life.
- *Following the Master: Discipleship in the Steps of Jesus* by Michael J. Wilkins (Zondervan). An insightful discussion of the nature of discipleship in the first century and how it is depicted in the New Testament.
- *The Cost of Discipleship* by Dietrich Bonhoeffer (Macmillan). A classic exposition of the Sermon on the Mount by a German pastor killed because of his opposition to Hitler.
- *Coloring Outside the Lines: Discipleship for the "Undisciplined"* by John F. Westfall (Harper-San Francisco), 1991. An unusual but very refreshing look

at Christian discipleship written by a self-described "night person" who contends that most discipleship books are written by "morning people." This is an attempt to provide a book for people who don't fit the mold.

◆ *In Search of Happiness: A Guide to Personal Contentment* by James Houston (Lion).

◆ *Taking Discipleship Seriously: A Radical Biblical Approach* by Tom Sine (Judson).

◆ *Disciplemakers' Handbook: Helping People Grow in Christ* by Alice Fryling, ed. (InterVarsity).

◆ *Essentials of Discipleship* by Francis Cosgrove (NavPress).

◆ *Jesus' Call to Discipleship* by James D.G. Dunn (Cambridge).

Reflection Questions

 The past can cripple us. Paul urges us to "forget" what lies behind. But we cannot forget until we remember. We need to face our past and then give it over to God, letting it go as we look to the future. It is the future that should motivate us (with all that God has promised us), not the past that hampers us (because we are weighed down by what has happened).

1. What, if anything, weighs you down from the past? What did you do? What happened to you? What choices did you make which you wish you could undo? By locating exactly where the pain lies, you can face it and deal with it. Do you need to process the past with someone: a friend, a minister, a counselor, or a therapist? What help do you need to leave the past behind?

2. What, if anything, motivates you for the future? Are you motivated more by the short-term (rewards in the near future) or by the long-term (what will be one day)? Does the hope of becoming like Christ motivate you? If so, how? If not, what do you need to do to let this motivate you? Does the hope of heaven motivate you? If so, how? If not, what do you need to do to let this motivate you?

3. How do you grow best? In spurts or gradually? Out of crisis or by careful attention to your unfolding life? Look back over the phases of your life and discern the changes that took place and how they came about.
   ▶ What spiritual understanding did you have as a child, and how did that grow (if at all)?
   ▶ What spiritual understanding did you have as a teenager, and how did that grow (if at all)?
   ▶ What spiritual understanding do you have as an adult, and how do you best grow?

4. What tends to be your first response to insight in an area of your life that needs to change: "yes" or "no"? How assured are you of God's love and willingness to forgive you? How has that affected your willingness to face what is ugly in your life and repent? To what degree does Scripture (as opposed to culture) determine your pattern for living? To what degree are you experiencing the power of fellowship and the Holy Spirit to change you?

5. Complete work on your testimony (see the *Optional Exercise* in *Understanding the Text*).

Journal

Chapter Seven
Being Ourselves

Overview

What we will become in Christ is quite breathtaking—new men and women made over in the image of Christ. Of course, we will never fully attain such a high goal in this lifetime. That must wait for the life to come in the "eternal kingdom" which Peter speaks of in the passage we will study. However, we can strive in that direction, making every effort to become what Jesus has declared we are. The Apostle Peter challenges us to do so.

We will explore this issue through study of a Bible passage in which the Apostle Peter describes what the Christian should strive to be (2 Peter 1:3–11); through a discussion of the mysterious word "holiness"; and by means of reflection on character development—past, present, and future.

The hope is that in the small group experience and through your own study, you will grow in your understanding of what it means to be a new person in Christ. This is what learning to love yourself is all about.

Beginning (20 minutes)

A Good Person

"You're a good man, Charlie Brown." Ever wonder what makes someone a good man or a good woman?

1. What do you think is the chief characteristic of a "good" person? What do you think is the second most important characteristic? Why?
   - ❐ kindness
   - ❐ compassion
   - ❐ honesty
   - ❐ integrity
   - ❐ humility
   - ❐ spirituality
   - ❐ wisdom
   - ❐ sense of humor
   - ❐ empathy
   - ❐ good deeds
   - ❐ fair and just
   - ❐ faithful
   - ❐ love
   - ❐ other: _____

2. Describe someone you know who qualifies as a genuinely "good" person. If you can, illustrate what you mean with a story about that person.

3. How much progress are you making at becoming a "good" person?
   - ❐ I'm still in the driveway.
   - ❐ My car won't start.
   - ❐ I'm on the freeway.
   - ❐ I'm making good time but I'm lost.
   - ❐ I've arrived.
   - ❐ I've driven a few blocks.
   - ❐ I'm driving around in circles.
   - ❐ I'm in the breakdown lane.
   - ❐ I see my exit straight ahead.

The Text

Everything that goes into **a life of pleasing God** has been **miraculously given to us** by **getting to know**, personally and intimately, **the One** who invited us to God. The best invitation we ever received! We were also given absolutely terrific promises to pass on to you—your tickets to **participation in the life of God** after you **turned your back on** a **world** corrupted by lust.

So **don't lose a minute** in building on what you've been given, **complementing** your basic **faith** with **good character, spiritual understanding**, alert discipline, **passionate patience, reverent wonder**, warm friendliness, and **generous love**, each dimension fitting into and developing the others. **With these qualities** active and growing in your lives, no grass will grow under your feet, no day will pass without its reward as you **mature** in your **experience of our Master Jesus**. Without these qualities you **can't see what's right before you**, oblivious that your old sinful life has been wiped off the books.

So, friends, **confirm God's invitation** to you, his choice of you. Don't put it off; do it now. Do this, and you'll have your life on a firm footing, the streets paved and the way wide open into the eternal kingdom of our Master and Savior, Jesus Christ.

2 Peter 1:3–11
Eugene H. Peterson/The Message

Understanding the Text (20 minutes)

We are all called to be "good" people. Peter helps us to understand what the life of a good person looks like and how we can possess it.

1. Explore the opening part of this passage (paragraph one) by answering the following questions:
   ▶ What is our source of power for living the Christian life?
   ▶ What are the characteristics of that power?
   ▶ What two promises does Peter mention here?

2. Explore the next section (paragraph two) by answering the following questions:
   ▶ What are the eight virtues we are to exhibit in our lives?
   ▶ Define each of these virtues.
   ▶ How does each virtue build on the preceding one?
   ▶ What is the fruit of these virtues?
   ▶ What does the lack of these virtues indicate?

3. Explore the final section (paragraph three) by answering the following questions:
   ▶ How can we be sure we are part of God's kingdom?
   ▶ What is the outcome of such a life?

4. Discuss the following description of the "tree of faith" found in verses 5–7:
   "Each step gives birth to and facilitates the next. Each subsequent quality balances and brings to perfection the one preceding."[1]

Optional Exercise

What would be the unique characteristic of a person who epitomized each of the virtues named by Peter? That is, what would be distinctive about a person of...

- ▶ faith?
- ▶ goodness?
- ▶ knowledge?
- ▶ self-control?
- ▶ endurance?
- ▶ godliness?
- ▶ mutual affection?
- ▶ love?

Which of the above characteristics would you like for the important people in your life? Pick the most important characteristic for each of the following people:

- ▶ roommate
- ▶ spouse
- ▶ son or daughter
- ▶ used-car salesman
- ▶ minister
- ▶ best friend
- ▶ brother-in-law

Applying the Text (20 minutes)

1. Explore the personal implications of the first section:
   - ▶ How do we tap into the power of God in our lives?
   - ▶ What is the "corruption" from which we must escape?
   - ▶ What does it mean for you to "participate in the divine nature"?

2. On one hand, Peter says that God's "divine power has given us everything needed for life and godliness" (verse 3). On the other hand, he says we are to "make every effort" to add all these virtues to our lives (verse 5).
   - ▶ What is the relationship between God's action and our efforts?
   - ▶ What is the outcome in people's lives when they passively wait for God to do it all?
   - ▶ What is the outcome in people's lives when they feel it is up to them to do it all?
   - ▶ In what ways have you experienced this tension in your life between these two realities?

3. Of the eight virtues in the second paragraph (see list in *Optional Exercise* above):
   - ▶ Which are the easiest for you to live out (don't be modest)? Explain.
   - ▶ Which are the hardest (don't be hesitant)? Explain.
   - ▶ Which one is the most challenging to you in your life at this point in time (don't be shy)? Explain.

4. Discuss the following statement: "Our virtues do not earn us heaven; they demonstrate that heaven is in us."

5. In what concrete ways are you trying to possess these qualities in increasing measure? In other words, how do you seek to grow in your Christian life?

Optional Exercise

For each of the eight virtues, discuss how you would construct a church-based Sunday school curriculum to teach these to a particular group of students. Choose a specific age for the students you want to teach.

Bible Study Notes

Setting: Peter begins by establishing the basis for the Christian life in what God has done for us in Christ. He then exhorts Christians to live a life of character. He identifies eight virtues they are to exhibit.

a life of pleasing God: Other translations say "a godly life." "Godliness" means a respect for God's will and God's way of life.

miraculously given to us: It is God's divine power that enables us to live the Christian life.

by getting to know...the One: The source of this divine power is Jesus. The reference is not merely knowledge about God (doctrine), but also about personal knowledge through our relationship with Jesus. Other translations include the words "glory" and "goodness" to define the excellence of Jesus. The word "glory" (shining, brightness, radiance) points to Jesus' inner being in all its attributes, while the word "goodness" points to his deeds and moral excellence (which express his inner being).

participation in the life of God: We are called upon not only to turn away from corruption but to turn toward the divine nature. Believers enter into a relationship with the Godhead. They know God the Father, they become one with God the Son, and they are indwelt by God the Holy Spirit. Elsewhere in the NT, this idea is expressed in terms such as being born again (John 3:3; 1 Peter 1:23); being the temple of the Holy Spirit (1 Corinthians 6:19), and being in Christ (one of Paul's favorite terms, e.g., Romans 8:1).

turned your back on: By the power and promises of God and the person of Jesus, we can flee from our corrupt, sinful natures.

world: Society which is alienated from God, because it has rebelled against God.

don't lose a minute: Also translated, "make every effort." While it is true that the power for the Christian life comes from God, it is also true that we are to make every effort to live out the Christian life.

complementing: "Generous and costly co-operation. The Christian must engage in this sort of co-operation with God in the production of a Christian life which is a credit to him" (Green).

faith: This is the first of eight virtues which Peter has selected as representative of a healthy Christian life. Faith is the God-given ability to trust Christ; it is our response of acceptance of the love of God which is offered to us.

good character: "Excellence." We are called upon to live good lives; excellent lives that bear the mark of Jesus; Christlikeness.

spiritual understanding: We need to have a clear sense of who God is and what his way is (as revealed in Scripture).

passionate patience: Perserverance ("keeping on") is an important virtue. The Christian is called to withstand both opposition and enticement.

reverent wonder: Respect of God and his ways. This will determine the choices we make.

generous love: *Agape* is a selfless giving for the sake of others and is to be extended to all people.

With these qualities: Christians already possess these qualities. Their job is to manifest them in ever-increasing fashion.

mature: Our goal is to become more closely conformed to the portrait Peter has painted here of the Christian life. No one will ever fully succeed in possessing all of these virtues to full measure. Rather, they define the direction our growth must take.

experience of our Master Jesus: We will never fully grasp Jesus in this life. We must grow constantly in understanding and relationship.

can't see what's right before you: Those who do not manifest these character traits are spiritually blind, lacking insight, and under the influence of the world.

confirm God's invitation: It is not that cultivation of virtues makes a person part of the kingdom (Christ's death on the cross does that). These fruits are simply evidence of the divine reality in their lives.

Comment

That Mysterious Word "Holiness" *by John White*

Two ideas are paramount when the Bible talks about God's holiness, an attribute which more than any other seems to express the essence of what God is. One idea has to do with separateness and difference. God is wholly unlike anything we can conceive or know. He is infinitely greater and more powerful besides being qualitatively utterly dissimilar from us and from the universe he created. Though we are made in his image, and therefore reflect his being, the difference is such as to create a chasm of endless depth between what he is and what we are. "I am what I am," says God, "and there is nothing with which I can be compared."

The second idea has to do with morality. Bound up in the qualitative difference I have mentioned is ultimate ethical beauty and moral perfection. God's holiness is not merely total separation from uncleanness but a positive goodness beyond our capacity to conceive. The very heavens are unclean in his sight. Yet it is this same goodness and beauty which he wants to share with you. He wants you to be like him.

You will never understand him, yet you are called to know him. You are different from him, yet he wants to give you the quality which most distinguishes him from you. You are redeemed to be set aside for God's special use and made a partaker of his moral perfection.

Knowing him and sharing his holiness are closely related. "Who shall ascend the hill of the Lord? And who shall stand in his holy place? He who has clean hands and a pure heart" (Psalm 24:3–4). Only pure eyes can see him and that but dimly. Yet if you but catch a glimpse of him, he will share his beauty with you so that your face, like that of Moses, will shine with glory.

It would be nice if I could say about this chapter what I have already said about other passages: Skip it if you're not interested. But holiness is not optional for the Christian. It is not an elective. It is your major. The command rings out from across the yawning gulf, "Be ye holy for I am holy." Impossible as the command may seem, you have no choice but to obey it. "This is the will of God, your sanctification" (1 Thessalonians 4:3). You are left with no say in the matter. It is the will of God that you be holy, and be holy you must (Romans 6:22; 12:1; Ephesians 1:4; 1 Thessalonians 3:13; 4:7; 2 Timothy 1:9; 1 Peter 1:15; 2:5; 2 Peter 3:11)....

When you became a Christian, God did much more than forgive your sins. He made you righteous. He, the judge of dead and living, pronounced you, "Not guilty!" He now looks upon you and behaves toward you as though you were perfectly righteous. He does not deceive himself about you. Rather, your hand is held by the hand of the Christ who redeemed you by his blood. "This one is mine!" Jesus cries. "I have paid for every one of his transgressions." "It is well!" the reply comes back from the throne. "For such as he I sent you to suffer. Henceforth let there be peace between him and me. Welcome, ransomed child of mine; your sins are blotted out as the sun by a thick cloud. I will remember them no more."

But God did more than justify you. He sanctified you. Not content with declaring your righteous, he began to share his holiness with you. "Not with me," you may say. "I only wish I could be sanctified. It is one thing to know I am justified. It is quite another to claim I am sanctified." Yet the Scriptures insist on both. They are two sides of the same coin. Unless you grasp their intimate relationship, you will enjoy neither the peace of justification nor the joy and freedom of sanctification. To separate them is to mutilate both.[2]

The Art of Bible Study

Coming to Conclusions

The process of interpretation ends when we are able to state what a passage means. Now, of course, we seldom fully understand a passage (much less explore it in all of its depth). This is why we continue to study the Bible our whole life. Still, the aim of our Bible study is to come to some conclusions about a passage (through interpretation) and having done so, to be able to state these conclusions.

There are various ways to state what a passage means:

▶ *Summary Paragraph:* Perhaps the most straightforward way of expressing your conclusions is simply by writing out what you think the passage means.

For example, what Peter seeks to do in 2 Peter 1:3–11 is to exhort the recipients of his letter to grow in Christian virtues. He begins by encouraging them with the fact that it is God's power that will enable them to live a godly life. (God's power reflects his very nature, which we can participate in as we flee the corruption in the world.) Peter then names eight virtues, which build upon one another, and shows that possessing these virtues deepens our relationship with Jesus. He ends by pointing out that exhibiting these virtues is a sign that we are in the kingdom of God.

▶ *Paraphrase:* Try restating the passage in your own words, as for example, in a letter to a friend. You could try writing a paraphrase of 2 Peter 1:3–11 in the form of a letter to your daughter as she goes off to college, urging her to continue growing in her Christian life.

▶ *Outline or Sentence Diagram:* This is a more formal (or technical) way of revealing the meaning of a passage.

For example, the *NIV Study Bible* outlines this passage as follows:
II. Exhortation to Growth in Christian Virtues (1:3–11)
    A. The Divine Enablement (1:3–4)
    B. The Call for Growth (1:5–7)
    C. The Value of Such Growth (1:8–11)

▶ *Chart:* Each piece of writing has a logic to it. It is useful to draw charts (especially for longer passages) which visually show the connection between the parts of the passage and illustrate the logic behind the connection.

However you do it, state your conclusions about the passage. If you cannot do this, you have not completed the interpretation process.

Extra Reading

These books deal with the subject of holiness. This is not a widely used term today, but it is a biblical concept that needs to be rediscovered. Some of these books deal with the related subject of character formation.

- *Christian Character: Becoming the Person God Wants You to Be* by Andrea Sterk and Peter Scazzero (InterVarsitys). A series of Bible studies on themes such as servanthood, humility, and perseverance.
- *A Heart for God* by Sinclair Ferguson (NavPress).
- *The Pursuit of Holiness* and *The Practice of Godliness,* both by Jerry Bridges (NavPress).
- *The Power of Commitment* by Jerry White (NavPress).
- *Christian Spirituality: Five Views of Sanctification* by Donald Alexander, ed. (InterVarsity). Different denominations have understood spirituality in different ways. The book consists of essays from five perspectives along with responses.
- *Holiness: Its Nature, Hindrances, Difficulties, and Roots* by J. C. Ryle (James Clarke).
- *The Way of Holiness: A Study in Christian Growth* by Kenneth Prior (InterVarsity).
- *Invitation to Holiness* by James Fenhagen (Harper & Row).
- *The Call to Holiness: Spirituality in a Secular Age* by Martin Parsons (Eerdmans).
- *Christian Holiness* by Stephen Neill (Harper).

Reflection Questions

What kind of person do you want to become? Use your *Journal* to reflect on this question.

1. Before you can consider what you want to become, you need to know who you have been. Take each of the eight virtues and ask yourself the following question:
   ▶ Were a good friend (one who is both honest and compassionate) to describe how well you matched up to each of the eight virtues in your pre-conversion days, what would he or she say about you?

2. Now answer the same question about yourself in the here and now:
   ▶ What are your strong points and weak points when it comes to the eight virtues?

3. With these past and present perspectives in mind, sketch out the kind of progress you want to make in your life. What must you do to become this sort of person? Do not be too harsh on yourself nor too impatient. Character building is a lifelong process.

---

[1]Michael Green, *2 Peter and Jude* (Eerdmans, Tyndale NT Commentaries, 1972), quoting Bengel, page 80.

[2]Taken from *The Fight* by John White (InterVarsity, 1976), pages 180–182.

Journal

The Art of Leadership
Brief Reflections on How to Lead a Small Group

It is not difficult to be a small group leader. All you need is:

◆ The willingness to do so;
◆ The commitment to read through all the materials prior to the session (including the leader's notes for that session);
◆ The sensitivity to others that will allow you to guide the discussion without dominating it;
◆ The willingness to have God use you as a small group leader.

Here are some basic small group principles that will help you to do your job.

Ask the questions: Your role is to ask the group to respond to each of the questions in the study guide. Simply read the questions and let various group members respond.

Guide the discussion: Ask follow-up questions (or make comments) that draw others into the discussion, and keep the discussion going. For example:

◆ "John, how would you answer the question?"
◆ "Anybody else have any insights into this question?"
◆ "Let's move on to the next question."

Start and stop on time: Your job is to start the group on time and (most importantly) to stop it on time. Certain people will always be late, so don't wait until they arrive. Make sure you end on time. If you don't, people will be hesitant to come again since they never know when they will get home.

Stick to the time allotted to each section: There is always more that can be said in response to any question. So if you do not stick very carefully to the time limits for each section, you will never finish the study. And this usually means the group will miss out on the very important application questions at the end of the session. It is your job to make sure that the discussion keeps moving from question to question. You may have to keep saying: "Well, it is time to move on to the next question." Remember: it is better to cut off discussion when it is going well than to let it go on until it dies out.

Model answers to questions: Whenever you ask a question to which everyone is expected to respond (for example, a *Beginning* question as opposed to a Bible study question), you, as leader, should be the first person to answer. In this way, you show others the right amount of time to respond. If you take 5 minutes to respond, everyone else in the group will feel that it is okay for them to take at least 5 minutes (so one question will take 50 minutes for the whole group to answer!). But if you take one minute to answer, so will everyone else (and the question takes only 10 minutes for the group to answer). Also, by responding first, you model an appropriate level of openness. Remember, the leader should be just a little bit more open than others.

Understand the intention of different kinds of questions: You will ask the group various kinds of questions. It is important for you to understand the purpose of each kind of question:

◆ *Experience questions:* These are often the first type of questions you will ask. The aim of these questions is to cause people to recall past experiences and share these memories with the group. There is no right or wrong answer to these questions. Such questions facilitate the group process by:
- getting people to share their stories with one another.
- being easy to answer, so everyone has something to say and thus the group conversation begins.
- getting people to think about the session topic on the basis of their own experience.

◆ *Forced-choice questions:* Certain questions will be followed by a series of suggested answers (with check-boxes next to each possible answer). Generally, no particular answer is correct. In fact, often each answer is correct. By offering options, group members are aided in responding. This also helps direct the response. When people answer such questions, you may want to ask them to explain why they chose the answer they did.

◆ *Analysis questions:* These are questions that force the group to notice what the biblical text says and to probe it for meaning.

◆ *Application questions:* These questions help the group make connections between the meaning of the text and each person's life circumstance.

◆ *Questions with multiple parts:* Sometimes a question is asked and then various aspects of it are listed below. Have the group answer each of the sub-questions. Their answers, taken together, will answer the initial question.

Introduce each section: It is your job to introduce each section. This may involve:
- ◆ *Overview:* Briefly explain the focus, purpose, and/or topic of the new section.
- ◆ *Instructions:* Explain how to do the exercise.

Comments: Occasionally it will be helpful to the group if you bring into the discussion some useful information that you have discovered from your own study. Never make long comments. Do not allow yourself to become the "expert" whom everyone turns to for "the right answer." Invite comments from others.

Some comments about how the small group discussion is structured in this book:

There are four parts to each small group session, and each has a different aim:

◆ *Beginning:* The purpose of this section is to:
- Help people to move from the worries and concerns they brought with them (to the group) to the topic itself.
- Start people thinking about the topic in terms of their own experiences.
- Start discussion among group members.
- Encourage people to tell their stories to each other so they get to know one another.

◆ *Reading the Text:* The purpose of this section is to:
- Start the process of analyzing the text.
- Let people hear what they will then study. Reading helps people to notice things in the text they might not see otherwise.
- Focus on the text as the core of the small group study.

♦ *Understanding the Text:* The purpose of this section is to:
  • Immerse people in the text, so that they start to see what is there (the observation process).
  • Discern the main points of the text.
  • Understand the text as first-century hearers might have understood it.
♦ *Applying the Text:* The purpose of this section is to:
  • Understand what the text is saying (the interpretation process).
  • Apply the text to people's lives (the application process).

Begin each new session by:
♦ *Welcoming everyone.*
♦ *Opening in prayer:* Your prayer does not need to be long or complex. You can write it out beforehand. In your prayer, thank God for his presence. Ask him to guide the group into new wisdom, and to give each person the courage to respond to the text. You do not have to be the one who always opens in prayer. You can ask others to pray. It is usually a good idea to ask beforehand if a person is willing to pray aloud.
♦ *Introducing the topic:* Take no more than one minute to do this. Simply identify what you will be discussing, the text you will be studying, and the main ideas you will be examining. You will find this introductory material on the first page of each chapter.

Move to the *Beginning* exercise:
♦ Read the brief introduction aloud (when there is one), or just introduce the theme of the exercise.
♦ Give people a minute to read over the questions and think about their answers.
♦ Then as leader, begin the sharing by giving your answer to the first question:
  • Remember, there are no "right" answers—only personal stories or preferences.
  • Laughter is great medicine. These questions are seldom serious and invite funny stories (often from childhood).
♦ Move to the person on your right and ask him or her to respond.
♦ Go around the circle, so each person has a chance to respond to the question.
♦ Move to question 2 and do the same thing.
♦ Finish up with question three.
♦ Watch the time carefully so everyone has a chance to respond:
  • Don't worry if you do not get through all three questions, as long as people have started sharing.
  • After a few sessions, you will know how many questions you can get through with your group. You may need to pre-select one or two questions to use for this sharing time.
♦ Remember that even though this is lighthearted sharing, you are discussing the topic of the Bible study. Remind people of the theme of the subject.

Move to the second section of the small group study—*Understanding the Text:*
♦ Introduce the Bible passage by reading aloud (or summarizing in your own words) the introduction to this section.
♦ Read the Bible passage (or invite someone else to read it).
♦ Give the group a few minutes to read over the passage, read through the questions (and think about the answers), and to consult the *Bible Study Notes.*

- ◆ Ask question 1:
  - Get responses from several people.
- ◆ When you feel that the question has been sufficiently discussed, move to the next question.
  - In this section, some of the initial questions are fact-oriented. There are specific answers to them. Subsequent questions will be more open-ended and will invite discussion.
- ◆ Work through all of the questions:
  - Be sure you have worked through the questions yourself beforehand, so that you know which are the important questions that need more time.
- ◆ If you still have time left for this section, use the optional question (where there is one). These invite a lot of discussion and personal sharing that will fill the remaining time.
  - You may decide to skip some questions and end with the *Optional Question or Exercise.*
- ◆ Remember: your aim in this section is to help the group notice what the text says and to begin to interpret it.

Move to the final section of the small group study—*Applying the Text:*
- ◆ Follow the same discussion process as the *Understanding the Text* section.
- ◆ Remember: your aim in this section is to help the group grasp the meaning of the text and to apply it to their lives.

Conclude the small group session:
- ◆ Discuss the *Personal Study* section for the coming week:
  - Encourage people to read over the *Bible Study Notes* (if they have not had time to do so during the small group).
  - Encourage the group to read the *Comment* section.
  - Encourage people to study and then work on the ideas in *The Art of Bible Study* section.
  - Encourage people to do *Journal* work.
- ◆ End with prayer together.

Serve coffee, tea, soft drinks, etc.:
- ◆ This will give people a chance to talk informally.
- ◆ There is often very good conversation following a small group session, as people hash over the discussion.

Additional Exercises: There are a number of ways to enrich your small group session. You may want to add an extra exercise each week (e.g., start off each session with *Journal* sharing). Or you can vary the nature of the extra exercise (e.g., one week do a case study; the next week do a book report, etc.). What follows are suggestions for alternative or additional small group exercises.

Sub-Groups: You may want to divide the group into sub-groups of four for part of the sharing. This allows more time for each person to participate. Also, people who might be intimidated in a group of twelve find it easier to talk in a group of four.

- ◆ It is best to begin and end the session with everyone together.
- ◆ Do not form permanent sub-groups. Each week, have a different foursome meet together in a sub-group. In this way you maintain the identity of the whole group.

Journal: You may want to set aside time each week for people to share from their *Journals.* This can be a very powerful experience—you will discuss on a deep level the personal meaning of the previous week's passage.
- ◆ It is probably best to do this at the beginning of the session before you get into the new material.

Book Report: Bring along one (or more) of the books in the *Extra Reading* section:
- ◆ Discuss the content of the book.
- ◆ Ask someone else to discuss one of the books.

Comment: You may want to focus on the *Comment* section.
- ◆ Give people time to read it over (or read it aloud).
- ◆ Prepare questions that will enable the group to discuss the ideas in the *Comment* section.

Bible Study Notes: Some weeks you may want to spend time on these notes as a way of deepening the understanding of the text.
- ◆ You can do this by allowing more time for individual study of the text. Group members can then think about how they would answer each study question in light of the information in the notes.

The Art of Bible Study: It will be helpful to go over the process of Bible study from time to time—to encourage people to read and analyze the Bible on their own.
- ◆ Have someone report to the group about their experience in using some of these techniques.
- ◆ Make comments occasionally about *how* the group is analyzing the text at that moment. By doing this, you will highlight certain Bible study principles.

Sharing: Each week, ask a different person in the group to take five minutes and share how he or she came to faith. Or ask people to share how they applied biblical insights (from the previous study) to their lives during the week.

Case Study: Tell the actual story of somebody you know (or read about) and then ask the group: How can the principles we have studied in this text help in this situation?

Small Group Leader's Guide
Notes on Each Session

If you are the small group leader, it is important for you to read carefully the section entitled *The Art of Leadership: Brief Reflections on How to Lead the Small Group.* This will help you in the art of small group leadership. It will also give you ideas on how you can tailor the material to fit the needs of your specific group. Then prior to each session, go over the notes for that session (see below). These will focus on the specific materials in the session.

Chapter One: Loving Ourselves

1

Potluck: Since this is the start of a new (though related) topic, some groups will be starting up for the first time; other groups will be continuing after a break. If this is your situation, why not begin with a potluck supper as a good way to launch this new venture? See the comments on *Session One* in the *Learning to Love God* book for some tips about how to do this.

Introduction to the Bible Study: If your group is established already and has worked through *Learning to Love God,* your introduction to the new section can be brief. Simply identify the theme of the next seven sessions and how each session connects to it. If this is a new group, make sure that you introduce the nature and direction of the small group. You will want to touch on:

▶ *Series Theme:* In the seven small group sessions, you will be discussing what it means to learn to love ourselves. Thus you will be examining various issues concerning what it means to be a person who is following Jesus. Your aim will be to clarify the biblical understanding of human beings. Read the title of each session to the group.

▶ *Group Process:* In each session, you will begin with a brief time of sharing where the topic is introduced through experiences group members have had. Then you will study together a passage from the Bible, using the questions in this study guide. These questions will help you come to grips with what the passage means and how it applies to your lives.

▶ *Group Details:* Describe where you will meet, when, and for how long.

▶ *Group Aims:* The hope is that group members will grow in their understanding of what it means to know and love themselves in a proper way that avoids self-hatred or self-inflation; that they will apply these insights to their lives; and that they will begin to understand how to study the Bible on their own.

▶ *Prayer:* Pray briefly, thanking God for assembling this group. Ask God to guide your deliberations and sharing today and during the coming weeks. Pray that God will touch each life in such a way as to meet the deep needs of that person.

Beginning: One of the major themes in this chapter is self-image, or how we view ourselves. No one's self-image is created in a vacuum. Others help us to define ourselves. Sometimes this is good (when people love us, see us clearly, and help us recognize our distinctives). Other times this is bad (when people do not care for us, when they project bad images on us, and when they negate our personhood). What you want to get at in this opening exercise are the positive things said about us as children, (i.e., those comments and affectionate names that we like and that make us feel good about ourselves).

Be forewarned that some people have few, if any, positive memories of this kind from childhood. If people can't choose a name from the list, just move on in a lighthearted way to the next person. This is not the time to get into heavy issues from the past. (In *Chapter Seven,* we will be discussing how to deal with our past as new Christians.)

▶ *Question 1:* The focus is on terms of endearment.

▶ *Question 2:* The focus shifts from words that made us feel good as children to the people who made us feel good.

▶ *Question 3:* This question moves the group into the topic for this session: how we view ourselves. All of us carry with us words or images from childhood that help to define us as adults. "What a clever boy" allows you to think of yourself as a "smart" man. "What pretty pictures you paint" allows you to think of yourself as a creative woman.

Understanding the Text

▶ *Overview:* The theme of the passage is the meaning of the Great Commandment. You will want to make sure everyone understands how central this is to the teaching of Jesus. However, the main focus in this session is on one aspect of the Great Commandment: the comment by Jesus about loving ourselves. So begin the discussion in general terms, but make sure you get to the focus: the nature of proper self-love.

▶ *The Text:* There are various ways of presenting the passage. It is probably best to have someone read it aloud. Ask for a volunteer or read it aloud yourself. (Never ask a person to read aloud without first getting permission to have him or her do so. Some adults have trouble with reading aloud.) Then give group members a few minutes to go over the passage on their own, looking over the questions and the *Bible Study Notes.*

▶ *Question 1:* This will force the group to identify key features of the passage.

▶ *Question 2:* Make sure people see clearly how all-encompassing our love for God is meant to be.

▶ *Questions 3 and 4:* These will generate good discussion as people wrestle with what the text is saying. These questions will begin the interpretation process.

▶ It does not occur to some people that one's religious life and one's relational life have any connection. And yet, so much of the NT is about relationships between people. The Bible is filled with very practical insights into relationships.

▶ Likewise, few people connect self-love with loving others. Explore together the fact that how you feel about yourself shapes how you feel about others.

▶ *Question 5:* This question cannot be answered without reference to the context of this passage. See the *Bible Study Notes.*

▶ *Optional Question:* The aim of this exercise is to throw into sharp relief the amazing nature of the Great Commandment. Everybody has a functional philosophy. They may not be able to put this into words, but the decisions they make reveal their life philosophy. The central philosophy of life that

Jesus teaches leads to wholeness of life. This cannot be said about many other philosophies. You might want to ask the group to suggest other functional philosophies and so expand the list given in the book.

Applying the Text

▶ *Question 1:* It is important for the group to grasp what the Greek word *agape* means and how it contrasts with other definitions of love. See C. S. Lewis' book *The Four Loves* for more insight into this definition. One test of a person's definition of love is whether by that definition it is possible to love those you do not like (i.e., your enemies)! It is possible to love our enemies (as Jesus commands us to do) when we understand love to be *agape*.

▶ *Questions 2 and 3:* Try to make practical the concept of wholehearted love of God.

▶ *Question 4:* It is hard for some people to see how their religious life connects to their relational life. Yet this is a key point that Jesus makes here. Try to get practical illustrations of the nature of this connection. For example, in the Sermon on the Mount, Jesus tells us not to look at others with lust. Thus because of our commitment to following (and obeying) Jesus, we relate to men and women in a new way which is different than our society's way (which permits—and even encourages—lust).

▶ *Question 5:* This is the crucial question in this chapter. Save enough time to wrestle with these questions so that the group comes away with a good understanding of what proper self-love is and is not. This question makes the connection between proper self-love and the love of others. It is not always obvious what difference proper self-love makes to the love of others. See the *Reflection Questions* in the *Personal Study* section for examples of how this connection is made. You may decide to discuss one or two of these questions within this group of questions.

▶ *Question 6:* In order to love yourself properly, you must know yourself.

▶ *Optional Exercise:* This exercise connects with *question 6* by asking people to think about who they are. You will often find that the hardest part of this exercise is naming strengths. People are often well aware of weakness (and guilty about it), but are not in touch with the positive sides of who they are (and what they are able to bring to their relationships, work, ministry, etc.). This is a good small group exercise, since in naming strengths and weaknesses to others, we are owning these in a new way. If you do not have time to do this exercise, you can assign it as homework.

Concluding Issues

▶ *Group Covenant:* If this is the initial meeting of this group, have them turn to the section entitled *How to Use It: Questions About the Study Guide* (page 12). Give the group a few minutes to look over the Group Covenant. Discuss the group ground rules. Make sure everyone is comfortable with these ground rules. End by going around the group and giving each person an opportunity to agree to the final Group Covenant.

▶ *Group Invitation:* If your first session is a "trial meeting," invite all who attended to return next week for *chapter 2*. Returning for the second week will signal that they are committed for the duration of the series (six more weeks). If you have room in the small group (i.e., there are less than twelve people), encourage group members to invite friends for the second session.

After week two, no new members can join the group (since each time a new person comes it is necessary to rebuild the sense of community).

▶ *Group Homework:* Some groups may ask members to prepare certain materials for the next session. If you decide to do this, go over the homework at this point. You might want to ask people to work through the *Comment* section and put their observations in their journals. Or perhaps you can ask each person to be prepared the following week to share a brief *Journal* entry.

▶ *Group Prayer:* End with a time of prayer. Pray in a way that is comfortable for your group (i.e., you, as leader, may lead in prayer, ask someone to pray, let various people pray briefly as led by God, etc., depending upon the group).

Other Materials

▶ If this is the first session it will probably be useful to the group for you to go over the *Study Resources* and *Personal Study* sections of the book so everyone knows how these fit into the whole course.

▶ *Bible Study Notes:* Sometimes there is not enough time during the small group to do anymore than glance at these notes. In this case, it would be helpful for people to read them carefully on their own as a way of deepening their understanding of the text.

▶ *Comment:* The essays on self-love will provide more data for discussion. But if the *Comment* section is not used in the small group session it can be studied during the week by each individual.

▶ *The Art of Bible Study:* A person who reads these carefully will (over the course of the twenty-one sessions in the three books) learn the fundamentals of the inductive Bible study process. The hope is that these insights will enable such a person to study the Bible more profitably on his or her own. The focus in this book in on the interpretation process in Bible study.

▶ *Extra Reading:* Point out the variety of books that will allow further research on issues of interest.

▶ *Reflection Questions:* These will guide personal reflection in the *Journal* section. They may also be used as small group discussion questions.

▶ You may want to use some of this material as homework, which will be discussed in the next session.

Session Two: Valuing Ourselves

2

Overview

▶ *Welcome:* Greet the group and let them know how glad you are that they are all there. If this is a new small group, this means they have decided to be part of the group for the next six weeks. Tell them how much you are looking forward to your time together.

▶ *Prayer:* Pray briefly, thanking God for what he is doing in each person's life and asking him to guide your deliberations and sharing today. Pray that during this session God will make it crystal clear to each person where they fit into God's scheme of things (as against how culture defines and values—or devalues—them).

▶ *Theme:* Refer people to the *Overview* to *chapter 2* and the issue that will be discussed today.

Beginning

▶ In the text, a comparison is made between the status of angels and the status of human beings. For the weight of this to sink in, it is important that people think a bit about the nature of angels. This exercise is a fun, low-key way of pondering angels. The discussion here is picked up in the *Option Question* in *Understanding the Text.*

▶ *Question 1:* We all have images of angels. Such images will vary from culture to culture. In America, these images are often the product of advertising and movies (mingled with classic art).

▶ *Question 2:* Picturing angels is one thing; responding to them is quite another!

▶ *Question 3:* This gets at our ideas about angels and where we got them.

Understanding the Text

▶ *Question 1:* This is a different sort of observation question from the ones you are used to. It asks people to search through the text and locate what is said about three subjects. These are the main subjects of the passage, so this search will force the group to notice the key elements of the passage. You might want to list (on a large piece of paper taped to the wall) the responses of the group about each subject. Then you can refer back to these insights in subsequent questions.

▶ *Question 2:* Psalm 8:4–6 was both true in its original context (it said something very important about the nature of humanity) and prophetic (it said something very important about the Messiah who would come in the future). It applies to both people and to Jesus. Furthermore, it is clear that humanity has failed to live up to its high calling, and that its destiny will be realized through Jesus.

▶ *Question 3:* The various sub-questions will help the group to understand the high calling we have as members of the human race.

▶ *Question 4:* These verses say a lot about the human condition (we are fallen men and women, given over to sin) and how Jesus rescued us from our plight (through his death, whereby he took upon himself our sins and paid the price for our sin—"atonement").

▶ *Question 5:* The kingdom of God came into being when Jesus became a human being (see Mark 1:14–15). But it has not come in fullness yet—not everyone recognizes Jesus for who he is, Satan is still active in this world (though, in reality, he has been defeated by Jesus). Therefore, we live in an in-between time: in between the first coming of Jesus (his Incarnation) and the Second Coming (when his kingdom will come in its fullness).

▶ *Optional Questions:* This continues the discussion in the *Beginning* section. The first question expands and consolidates insights about angels; the second does the same for our understanding of who people are in God's eyes; and the third applies these insights to everyday life. Help the group see that claiming our birthright (as creatures made in God's image) gives us a powerful, positive self-image. As a result, we are kinder to others and less defensive or aggressive than we would be if we held an erroneous self-image (i.e., that all of life is a mistake, and we live in a meaningless universe).

Applying the Text

▶ *Question 1:* The aim of this question is to list what this passage says about who God has made people to be. Notice that the group is asked to reflect on the implications of each assertion in two ways: (1) what each assertion means for the way we view ourselves, and (2) how we would live with this being the case. The hope is that people will grasp the wonder of who God has made us, and will see how a proper self-image impacts daily life. This question picks up from the final question in the *Optional Question* of *Understanding the Text.*

▶ *Question 2:* This question gets at the so-called "cultural mandate" in Genesis 1:26–28 (in which God entrusts humanity with subduing the earth and putting all in subjection to us). To be caretakers of the earth is a high and demanding calling which is still ours to fulfill.

▶ *Question 3:* Here you reflect on the mystery of salvation. Jesus needed to be fully human (and yet without personal sin) in order to pay the price for the sin of others. He needed to be fully divine in order to pay the price for not just one person but all of humanity.

▶ *Question 4:* This question cuts to the core of the unit: how our relationships of love (to self, others, and God) are affected by a true view of who God made us.

▶ *Question 5:* Jesus' humanity has immediate application for us. He know our temptations well. He successfully resisted temptation and therefore can help us when we are tempted to be less than we are meant to be.

▶ *Optional Exercise:* This is a creative way of making the central insights of this Bible study practical.

Concluding Issues

▶ Assign homework (if any) and conclude in prayer together. In your prayer, thank God for who he has made you to be—a being just a little lower than an angel. Ask God to help you live in a way that reflects this fact.

Other Materials

▶ You may want to use other sections from this chapter as part of your small group session.

▶ *The Art of Bible Study:* If your group is working on learning how to do Bible study, set aside some time to discuss the ideas in this section.

Session Three: Understanding Ourselves

3

Overview

▶ *Prayer:* Pray briefly—thank God for what he is doing in each person's life and ask God to guide your deliberations and sharing today. Pray that during this session, God will help you to understand our inclination to evil and how to deal with it.

▶ *Theme:* Refer people to the introduction to *chapter 3* and the issue that will be discussed today.

Beginning

▶ It is hard to admit that something in us is up to no good. We like the idea of being "a little less than angels." We do not like the idea that we may also have an evil virus in us. But we know this is true when we look at children. They are sweet, they are wonderful, they are innocent, they are lovable, and they can be disagreeable little mites. Something comes out at times that spoils all that niceness. Kids can't help it. They too are infected by the bad virus. We are going to look at the "naughty factor" in this lighthearted exercise. In the "kids-will-be-kids" breaking of rules, we catch a glimpse of the other principle.

▶ *Question 1:* This question asks about the kind of innocent mischief we got into as kids.

▶ *Question 2:* Of course kids eventually get caught, but they are masters at making up excuses.

▶ *Question 3:* Now as adults, we are victims of the same kinds of pranks we pulled on others when we were kids.

Understanding the Text

▶ *Question 1:* You might want to ask the group to circle "you" or "your" each time it is used in the passage. The original "you" was, of course, the Christians in Rome. But the words are addressed as powerfully to present-day readers. Help the group see that the passage is personal, addressed to each one of them.

▶ *Question 2:* Help the group begin to see the spiritual nature of our struggle to choose what is good, and that these choices also have spiritual consequences (death or righteousness).

▶ *Question 3:* The group should note words like "obedience," "reward," "wages," "servants," "service," "employed," and "duty" in this extended metaphor.

▶ *Question 4:* Each sub-question requires some reflection. You may want to refer to the *Bible Study Notes* for help. Get the group thinking about the transition from one master to the other and how this takes place (by responding to the teaching of Jesus). This transition (called conversion) is one of the subjects of *Book One: Learning to Love God.*

▶ *Question 5:* Help the group to see the difference between sin that pays out a just (though cruel) reward for service, and God who gives freely the wondrous gift of eternal life.

▶ *Optional Exercise:* This exercise can be very enlightening: considering different metaphors for sin and its impact on us. When we view sin as a disease, we see how it slowly takes over our body like cancer, impeding and frustrating all we do until it kills us. When we view sin as a twisted spring, we understand the negative impact of unbearable stress on us. If your group does not have the time (or the inclination) to write stories, then discuss the various metaphors and how each helps us to understand the nature and impact of sin.

Applying the Text

▶ *Question 1:* This is an extension and personalization of the *Optional Exercise* above, in that it moves the discussion from the metaphoric ("sin is like…") to the real ("This is how I experienced it."). The aim of the second sub-question is not to name these troubling areas (this will be done in the *Optional Exercise* in this section), but to identify the nature of the struggle.

▶ *Question 2:* This is the logical follow-up to *question 1.* Be sure, in both of these questions, not to draw the contrast so sharply between life without

Christ and life with Christ that you move out of reality into wishful thinking. Few people prior to conversion were truly evil, giving themselves completely to a life of sin. No one after conversion is fully righteous (since our sin nature, though crippled, is not dead). It is more a matter of direction and degree. We have shifted our life direction from following sin to following Jesus, and our actions are becoming more consistently "righteous."

▶ *Question 4:* In order to resist sin, we need to be conscious of it. While we might have been troubled by certain actions prior to conversion, we had little inclination or ability to resist temptation. As Christians, we need to recognize temptation in its many forms so that we can seek God's help in standing firm against it. Likewise, we need to be aware of the stirrings of good in us so as to be able to respond to them. This is a question with no "right" answer. Rather, it is worded so that the group can share their experiences.

▶ *Optional Exercise:* One of the ways we resist sin is by renouncing it. To name our sin is to mute some of its power over us. To name the sin of lying (or cheating or stealing or lust) is to bring that action out into the light of public scrutiny and accountability. You will know whether your group is ready for this kind of vulnerability. As leader, it will be up to you to begin the sharing and to set the tone for appropriate openness.

Concluding Issues

▶ Assign homework (if any) and conclude in prayer together. Pray that each person will be strengthened in his or her service to righteousness.

Chapter Four: Behaving Ourselves

4

Overview

▶ *Prayer:* Pray briefly—thank God for what he is doing in each person's life, and ask God to guide your deliberations and sharing today. Pray that during this session, you will develop a clear understanding of the Christian lifestyle.

▶ *Theme:* Refer people to the introduction to *chapter 4* and the issue that will be discussed today.

Beginning

▶ *Question 1:* This list of "virtues" is drawn from the text which the group will study. It is important for people to be able to acknowledge the good patterns in their lives. You can try a variation on this question. Instead of asking individuals to name their chief virtue, ask the group members to identify a virtue they see in each other. This can be quite affirming for everyone.

▶ *Question 2:* Keep this lighthearted. This is not time for confession. It is a chance to say: "And here is something, as you probably know, that I'm not very good about."

▶ *Question 3:* The sharing becomes positive again, with the focus on improving our virtues.

Understanding the Text:

▶ This is a somewhat more difficult passage to analyze than the ones we have looked at so far, because Paul packs a lot of information into a few verses. He begins by defining the change in behavior we are to make and the reason we can make it. Then he defines (in quite specific terms) the old behavior we are to flee and the new behavior we are to embrace. Your aim in this study is to unpack all the information here and apply it in practical ways to your lives. This is a passage that makes you work in order to understand it!

▶ *Question 1:* Paul begins by defining the reality which Christians live in: they are dead to the world and alive in Christ. This is reality. (Unfortunately, we will not fully realize this fact until the Second Coming of Jesus, when all ambiguity will be swept away. Then, for the first time, we can be fully who we are in Christ. Until that day, sin still trips us up.) Then Paul gives believers four imperatives (commands which they are to follow) which define the transition from the old life to the new life. The first two commands (which are positive) call believers to bring a new focus to their hearts and minds. The second two commands (which are negative) call believers to flee the old.

▶ *Questions 2 and 3:* Pool your knowledge about the definition of each negative and positive behavior. The *Bible Study Notes* will help. You might also want to consult a dictionary (either an ordinary dictionary or a Bible dictionary). In fact, you could bring along various dictionaries—divide the group into working teams, and ask each team to define certain words and phrases using a dictionary. Each group then reports back to the whole group. Since Bible dictionaries are introduced in the *Art of Bible Study* section, this exercise also serves to show their use and value.

▶ *Optional Exercise:* Each culture implicitly defines what is good and bad behavior. This cultural definition is different in certain ways from the biblical definition. In America, television both reflects and influences this implicit definition. This exercise asks people to examine our cultural definitions.

Applying the Text

▶ *Question 1:* We are dead to sin and alive in Christ, yet we still sin. This is the dilemma—how to live in this in-between time prior to Christ's return. The aim in the Christian life is to be what we are: to live as if we were dead to sin and alive to Christ.

▶ *Question 2:* This question builds on the first question and looks at various resources that assist us in living an effective Christian life. These resources will vary in significance to people at different times in their lives. Encourage honest group sharing of what helps people to say "No" to sin and "Yes" to Christ.

▶ *Question 4:* There are various ways to use this question depending on the time available. You may only be able to discuss, in general terms, the assertion about behavior and relationships. If possible, discuss how these behaviors affect relationships with specific people (such as spouses or parents). Or you can pick one behavior (e.g., rage or forgiveness) and think about its application with children (or friends). Be flexible, but encourage the group to see how these behaviors (in this passage) make a difference in the world of human relationships.

▶ *Optional Questions:* It is confusing to some how certain people who are openly anti-Christian can seem to live better lives than others who are Christians. The verse quoted here gives us insight into how this can be so. Because of differences in background and circumstances, some individuals are by nature able to live better, more moral lives than others. Now suppose that a rather unlikable individual from an unfortunate background becomes a Christian. Even though he is a Christian, his life will, at first, be lived on a lower level than a kindly pagan from a good home. This is because the new Christian has a lot "to learn about what he ought to be according to the plan of God." Becoming a Christian does not automatically make him perfect. This sort of person may appear worse than the good pagan, but he is still in the process of becoming what he ought to be. Judge a person's Christianity not by where he or she is morally, but by how much he has changed. (See *Mere Christianity*, Book IV, Chapters 10 and 11, for a fuller explanation of this idea.)

Concluding Issues
- ▶ Assign homework (if any) and conclude in prayer together. Pray that each person will experience anew the freedom of living the Christian life.

Chapter Five: Forgiveness for Ourselves

5

Overview
- ▶ *Prayer:* Pray briefly—thank God for what he is doing in each person's life, and ask God to guide your deliberations and sharing today.
- ▶ *Theme:* Refer people to the introduction to Chapter Five and the issue that will be discussed today.

Beginning
- ▶ *Questions 1 and 2:* We all have our weaknesses! In fact, the discussion here in this opening exercise is "indulgences" (rather than serious temptation). Still, overindulgence could be a real problem and a genuine temptation.
- ▶ *Question 3:* Now we get to the real thing—true temptation which leads to true sin. Different cultures have different temptations. It is useful to know your culture's temptations. Don't forget things like power, materialism, and selfishness.

Understanding the Text
- ▶ *Question 1:* The passage from 1 John is carefully written. Unless you notice how John has constructed these verses, you will not see clearly what he is saying. Make sure the group sees the symmetry of the passage.
- ▶ *Question 2:* John identifies the errors of the false teachers and then corrects them. Make sure the group can paraphrase what John says. If we can't put these assertions into our own words, we probably have not understood them.
- ▶ *Question 4:* It is crucial for the group to see that God will forgive us. It is in his nature. But we must ask for forgiveness ("confess our sin"). To ask for forgiveness requires that we acknowledge our sin and that we are sorry for it. But it is not our sorrow (or repentance) that brings forgiveness. It is Christ's death on the cross that paid the price for our sin.
- ▶ *Question 5:* This question probes the dynamics of temptation. The important things to see are: that everyone is tempted (nobody can claim exemption); that temptation itself is not sin (it is the giving in to temptation that is the sin); that we are promised sufficient strength to resist

temptation; and that there is always a way of escape we can choose.

▶ *Optional Question:* This should generate useful discussion about the struggles we all have (when it comes to mastering those drives and impulses that would lead us to sin).

Applying the Text

▶ *Question 1:* It is impossible to describe God. All we can do is use metaphors (as John does here) which hint at his nature. If you have time you might want to discuss the other metaphor for God that John uses in this letter: God is love (1 John 4:8).

▶ *Question 2:* This question looks at forgiveness from the point of view of broken relationships, where one person has sinned against another. The dynamics of forgiveness involve asking for forgiveness, extending forgiveness, and receiving forgiveness. Forgiveness is the way of dealing with the breakdown in human relationships. Underlying human forgiveness is divine forgiveness, which makes it possible both to give and to receive forgiveness. Unforgiven people find it hard to forgive others. The root of human forgiveness is divine forgiveness. Forgiven people can forgive others.

▶ *Question 3:* You should probably come up with examples ahead of time that will guide the group's thinking. For instance:

* Clergy would appear to be the last people to give in to sexual temptation. But, in fact, it is not uncommon to hear about affairs between a minister and a parishioner. Part of the problem is that clergy may feel they would never be tempted this way, and so they do not guard against it. Thus they are caught by lust before they know what is happening.
* We have all heard about alcoholics who one day sense God's grace, and are thereafter able to say "No" to alcohol.
* Escape can come through knowledge. A person who is aware of vulnerability is alert to warning signs that he or she is getting into a risky situation, and therefore takes evasive action.

▶ *Question 4:* Each of the options is a potential "way of escape" from sin. Use these as the basis for a discussion about dealing with temptation.

▶ *Optional Questions:* The first three questions probe forgiveness in the context of human relationships; the fourth, as it affects our relationship with God.

Chapter Six: Growing Ourselves

6 *Overview:* The hope of a heavenly prize drew Paul into the future with great determination. So too for us, future hope has great power to energize us in the present.

▶ *Question 1:* The excitement of children is contagious. For example, the future is so wondrous that even the naughtiest child will try to be better when Christmas looms on the horizon.

▶ *Questions 2 and 3:* We also experience the power of the future to energize us as adults. Your aim is to have the group express this energizing power of the future.

Understanding the Text

▶ *Question 1:* In terms of first-century Jewish religion, Paul stood at the pinnacle of spirituality. In both background and accomplishment, Saul (his pre-conversion name) was the epitome of spirituality.

▶ *Question 2:* To emphasize what he wants to say, Paul states and restates his point. Make sure the group notices the various ways Paul expresses his assessment of his pre-Christian accomplishments, what his goal in life is, and where righteousness is to be found.

▶ *Question 3:* Explore the image of the runner: straining forward mid-race, forgetting what is behind him, and conscious only of the prize which is ahead. Make sure the group notices that even though Paul was once conscious of his spiritual accomplishments (he had done it all by first-century Jewish standards), now he does not claim perfection. He is aware of how far he still has to go. Furthermore, note the dynamic expressed here ("press on"—twice; "straining toward") and the goal described ("prize"; the call of God; "heavenward").

▶ *Optional Exercise:* You may want to split up into sub-groups of four for this exercise. In this way, you will have adequate time for each person to share his or her testimony. Note that this exercise can be continued in the *Journal* exercises. Encourage group members to work on their testimonies during the time between small group sessions.

Applying the Text

▶ *Question 1:* Each person in the group will have a story to tell which is similar in some way to what Paul has shared.

▶ *Question 2:* The next three questions deal with different aspects of the dynamics of growth. This question probes our attitude to the past (we need to own up to our past, ask forgiveness of God and others, and let it go); to the present (we are called upon to strive forward; to be active in pursing growth); and to the future (we need to remember what we have been promised, lest we be discouraged).

▶ *Question 3:* This picks up on themes in *question 2* and probes the specifics of growth. The key point to be noted is that Paul urges an activism when it comes to growth (and that our ability to work at growth is related to the impact of the past and present on us).

▶ *Question 4:* This picks up on themes in *questions 2* and *3* and tries to highlight specific ways in which hope motivates us. For example, the promises that Jesus has taken hold of us as his own, that he wants us to become like him, and that he has given us resources for us to grow are a great encouragement to us. Likewise, the sure knowledge that one day we will be in heaven keeps us going when things get rough.

▶ *Optional Exercise:* Just as the metaphor of the runner highlights important aspects of the Christian life, so do other metaphors. As a group, think about each of the images (e.g., the role of the ambassador is to represent the king: he or she has no independent mandate, he or she strives to be a very faithful representative of the King, and their desire is not to bring disgrace on his name). Then note the parallels in the Christian life (e.g., we represent Jesus to the world around us, etc.). Three of the metaphors listed are used in Scripture: the pilgrim in Hebrews 11 and 12; the soldier in 2 Timothy 2:3–4; and the ambassador in 2 Corinthians 5:20.

Chapter Seven: Being Ourselves

Overview

- ▶ *Question 1:* It could be argued that each of these characteristics are part of a truly "good" person. However, do not let anyone get away with such an answer! The interesting thing will be the explanations of why particular traits are singled out.
- ▶ *Question 2:* Goodness is better illustrated than described. We all know genuinely good people. Their stories will illustrate what we should all strive to be.
- ▶ *Question 3* Few people will describe themselves as "good." The aim of the question is to get people to identify that becoming "good" is a process and we are all on the way.

Understanding the Text

- ▶ *Question 1:* Peter begins with an amazing assertion: the power to live the Christian life comes from God, it reflects his character, and brings with it the promise of the life we desire to lead.
- ▶ *Question 2:* This series of questions leads to the heart of the passage: the list of eight virtues that define the direction our growth as Christians should take.
- ▶ *Question 3:* The role of the virtues is explained. We do not earn a place in heaven by living this way. Rather, living this way is a demonstration that the life of God is in us and that we will, one day, know eternal life.
- ▶ *Question 4:* Your aim in discussion is to understand what Bengel (the author of the quotation) means by his statement. By understanding Bengel, the group will understand the flow of these verses.
- ▶ *Optional Exercise:* By examining what each characteristic looks like in the life of a person who displays it, you will make the virtues quite concrete. The second part of the question is a fun way to think about the kind of people we'd like to associate with.

Applying the Text

- ▶ *Question 1:* Divine power is a mysterious subject—this power is very real, and yet God will not be manipulated. It is *his* power—we cannot demand it from him. Wrestle with how God's power is known in our lives. Also think about what it means to participate in God's nature. Stay clear of any sense that we ourselves become divine. This is not what is meant here.
- ▶ *Question 2:* Explore the tension between God's action and our efforts in becoming the kind of people we are called to be.
- ▶ *Question 3:* Here the aim is to personalize the virtues and our struggle to exhibit them in our lives.
- ▶ *Optional Exercise:* This will give you a good opportunity to discuss with each other how to teach virtues. Pick an age which is familiar to you (young children, junior highs, teens, young adults, adults, etc.) and then discuss what you want to teach about each virtue and the way you would go about it. Keep your lessons practical and not just theoretical. As you reflect on how to communicate virtues to others, you will be surprised at what you, as potential teachers, learn. You will probably not have time to cover the teaching of more than one or two virtues, so choose the ones that are of the most interest to the group.

Farewell Party: Since this is the final session in this book, set aside some time to bring a formal conclusion to the series. Some of the things you might consider doing include:

▶ *Share memories:* Ask group members to recall the best moments in the group (as well as the worst moments!). What did they especially appreciate about the group? What did they learn?

▶ *Pray together:* Commit the whole series to God. Ask God to take all that you have learned and use it in your lives. Let this be an extended time instead of a brief concluding prayer. You might want to bring some prayers to use (from the *Oxford Book of Prayer*), or you might want to give people time to write out prayers they will pray. You can also discuss as a group what to pray about. In any case, let this be a time of praise, thanksgiving, and commitment.

▶ *Plan the next series of small group sessions:* You may want to take a one or two week break before you begin again (or you may need to take a longer break if Christmas, summer, or some other special time is coming). You may decide to continue meeting weekly. In any case, plan on doing Book Three of this series: *Learning to Love Others.*

• Decide whether to keep group membership the same or to invite new members. Some group members may not be able to attend the new series. Bid them farewell. Think about how you can recruit new members. Or you may decide that one or two of your group will form a new group to go through *Learning to Love God* or *Learning to Love Ourselves* again with new people.

• Decide how the next group will be led.

▶ *Have a party:* Arrange for the kind of food and drink that will produce a good celebration. Enjoy each other. After all, a party is all about being with friends in a relaxed atmosphere—and you have made new friends during these seven weeks (and have deepened old friendships).

SMALL-GROUP MATERIALS FROM NAVPRESS

BIBLE STUDY SERIES

Design for Discipleship
God in You
God's Design for the Family
Institute of Biblical
   Counseling Series

Learning to Love Series
Lifechange
Love One Another
Studies in Christian Living
Thinking Through Discipleship

TOPICAL BIBLE STUDIES

Becoming a Woman of Excellence
Becoming a Woman of Freedom
Becoming a Woman of Purpose
The Blessing Study Guide
Celebrating Life
Homemaking
Intimacy with God
Loving Your Husband

Loving Your Wife
A Mother's Legacy
Praying From God's Heart
Surviving Life in the Fast Lane
To Run and Not Grow Tired
To Walk and Not Grow Weary
What God Does When Men Pray
When the Squeeze Is On

BIBLE STUDIES WITH COMPANION BOOKS

Bold Love
Daughters of Eve
The Discipline of Grace
The Feminine Journey
Inside Out
The Masculine Journey
The Practice of Godliness
The Pursuit of Holiness

Secret Longings of the Heart
Spiritual Disciplines
Tame Your Fears
Transforming Grace
Trusting God
What Makes a Man?
The Wounded Heart
Your Work Matters to God

RESOURCES

Brothers!
How to Build a Small Groups Ministry
How to Lead Small Groups
Jesus Cares for Women
The Navigator Bible Studies
   Handbook

The Small Group Leaders
   Training Course
Topical Memory System
   (KJV/NIV and NASB/NKJV)
Topical Memory System:
   Life Issues

VIDEO PACKAGES

Bold Love
Hope Has Its Reasons
Inside Out
Living Proof

Parenting Adolescents
Unlocking Your Sixth Suitcase
Your Home, A Lighthouse